To: K...
From: ...
Merry ...
All our best you in your future!

We Love
You!

What's Your FUNCTION?

Working It Out with God

Aaron M. Basko

Foreword by Andy Chan

JUDSON PRESS
PUBLISHERS SINCE 1824
Join our mailing list for updates and special offers.
www.judsonpress.com/mailing_list.cfm

Interior design by Beth Oberholtzer.
Cover design by Wendy Ronga and Hampton Design Group.

Cataloging-in-Publication Data available upon request.
Contact cip@judsonpress.com.

Printed in the U.S.A.

First printing, 2014.

Contents

Foreword by Andy Chan   v

1. What's on Your Name Tag? The Function Concept   1

2. Help! I Think My Work Is Cursed! The Meaning, Misery, and Mystery of Work   12

3. Misbehaving on Purpose: Answering the "What? Question   26

4. It Is All God's Fault: Following a Purpose-full God   40

5. Armed and Dangerous: The Purpose Finder Assessment   53

6. Get Inspired: Answering the "Where?" Question   65

7. Your Earnings Equation: Answering the "How?" Question   79

8. Storming the Market: Use Your Function to Land Jobs for Life!   98

9. Surf Your Personality: Navigating Your Personality in Changing Times   114

10. Living from Your Function: Staying True to God's Design   134

Appendix: Practical Applications of Function in Organizations and in Parenting   153

Foreword

At some point in a person's life, almost everyone asks the question, "What was I born to do?"

What's Your Function? by Aaron Basko is an exceptional book that can help you answer that question—and go much deeper than the typical career, job-search, or self-assessment book. The author methodically guides you to consider who God created you to be, as well as to articulate your life purpose.

As a compassionate and experienced mentor, teacher, and coach of college students, working professionals, and organizations, Basko provides numerous valuable and creative exercises to help you understand your unique wiring—your purpose, values, interests, strengths, personality, as well as how you make decisions. These building blocks are the foundation to understanding yourself—which is the crucial first step for successful career and life management.

Basko will thoughtfully challenge you to embrace your unique self, especially the parts of yourself that you or others may have perceived as weakness or eccentric or even irritating—looking as far back as childhood. (It was a powerful awakening to realize that some of my own behaviors that were not valued when I was a child could actually be quite valuable now that I am an adult.)

As a reader, you will reflect on and unpack life experiences and personal relationships, which have all occurred while on your individual journey with God—whether you knew it or not. These life experiences—what Aaron calls "fingerprints"—will provide insight in unrealized ways and provide meaning and guideposts for defining your identity and path, as well as insightful themes and information to guide your future direction and decisions.

Although we wish the process were easy, we all face obstacles and challenges. These hurdles often come in the form of our culture, our own mindset, and the influential voices of loved ones. Most of us struggle with caring too much about what others think or expect of us. *What's Your Function?* will enable you to identify and name these issues. As a result, you will acquire the freedom necessary to forge your unique path while increasing your trust in God.

When I had the opportunity of running the career center at Stanford's Graduate School of Business, I created and taught a seminar called "Career and Life Vision." Defining your *core purpose* was a crucial aspect of the model. You can discern your purpose using Basko's novel assessment, "The Purpose Finder," and through reading the Bible, an approach I used in my own life. By defining and articulating your purpose, you will have a whole new way of seeing how all that you do can be aligned with your life purpose.

Basko's transformation of the cliché "Follow your passion" into "Find your Inspiration—the impulse that motivates a great mission" is accurate and empowering. I have always felt that "Follow your passion" is not very helpful advice. Many struggle to identify a single passion. In fact, most people have multiple passions, some of which do not translate into valued or desired work or earnings. Instead, it is *Inspiration* that has staying power.

What's Your Function? provides sage perspective and practical advice about not only how to make a life, but also how to make a living. At Wake Forest University, where I work, our goal is similar: to teach and equip students to become employable for life and to lead a life of purpose and meaning. Job security is not about picking the one job to last a lifetime, but rather about developing the competencies, connections, and clarity of purpose and direction to enable you to navigate the ever-changing, uncertain world of work.

Through Basko's guidance, we learn how to turn our *Purpose* and *Inspiration* into *Earnings,* while embracing the reality that God is ultimately in control of our lives, careers, and future. As a result, you'll be more prepared for whatever you face—and less anxious about your decisions, circumstances, and career path.

What's Your Function? also offers practical approaches and tools for exploring and evaluating potential career directions. This is an area where many job seekers get stuck. Through this book, you will learn how to break that impasse; in particular, Basko's Professional Development Test is a powerful tool to help you determine if a particular career will be ultimately fulfilling and satisfying for you.

Basko also provides excellent strategies and tactics to run a successful job search—whether you are attending college, changing your career, experiencing a midlife "crisis," or just seeking a better job. One of my favorite lines from the author is, "This whole book, and indeed much of my work, is about encouraging others to get a deeper understanding of the mysterious work that God has done and is doing in their lives." You will understand God's amazing grace and love for you and how God has uniquely created you. Without a doubt, this is a precious gift that Aaron Basko shares with us all in *What's Your Function?*

So, read the book! Not only will you find the job and career that was made for you, but will learn that God is your divine Headhunter (Psalm 3:5-6). As you do your part, the Lord will do his.

Andy Chan
Vice President, Personal & Career Development
Office of Personal & Career Development
Wake Forest University
Winston-Salem, North Carolina

We are not yet what we shall be,
but we are growing toward it,
the process is not yet finished, but it is going on,
this is not the end, but it is the road.
—Martin Luther[1]

NOTES

1. Martin Luther, *Defense of All the Articles,* Lazareth transl., as found in Grace Brame, *Receptive Prayer* (St. Louis, Chalice Press, 1985), 119.

CHAPTER 1

What's on Your Name Tag?

The Function Concept

Conjunction Junction, what's your function? —*SCHOOLHOUSE ROCK*[1]

Most of what I know of English grammar I learned from *Schoolhouse Rock*, the Saturday morning cartoon interlude that ran on ABC in the 1970s and 1980s. *Schoolhouse Rock* taught lots of topics—American history, science, and math—but it was the grammar songs that stuck with me. I found out that "A Noun Is a Person, Place, or Thing," learned that you can "Unpack Your Adjectives," and, of course, discovered that conjunctions connect sentence parts.[2] (You can view videos of these and other *Schoolhouse Rock* classics at https://www.schooltube.com/search/?term =schoolhouse+rock.)

It is a good thing that those catchy songs stuck with me, because I don't remember being taught grammar clearly in much of the rest of my schooling. Most of my English classes were about reading or literature surveys, rather than language mechanics, and they seemed to be based on the principle of osmosis. If my classmates and I were surrounded by language all the time, surely we would pick up on how to use it without the drudgery of diagramming sentences or identifying parts of speech.

When I started learning a foreign language, however, it was slow going. I loved using Spanish words, but I felt like I had to learn English over again in order to grasp how the words should be put together. It was as if I had no framework to hang anything on. It was then that the *Schoolhouse Rock* jingles came back to me, and it sunk in that words have functions. You can't use them interchangeably or sloppily (adverbs I learned from "Lolly, Lolly, Lolly, Get Your Adverbs Here"[3]) and still get your point across effectively. Different types of words are meant to do different things. They are tools, and each has a purpose.

Let me give a *Schoolhouse Rock* example. The song "Rufus Xavier Sarsaparilla" teaches about the importance of pronouns. We use pronouns every day, and yet seldom, if ever, think about how much they improve our language by condensing it.

The song introduces us to three characters: Rufus Xavier Sarsaparilla; his sister, Rafaella Gabriella Sarsaparilla; and the narrator, Albert Andreas Armadillo. Each of them discovers and adopts an animal—one a kangaroo, one an aardvark, and one a rhinoceros. They go on adventures hopping through the jungle and even riding on a city bus.

Along the way, poor Albert Andreas Armadillo just about expires because he has to keep repeating all of their ridiculously long names over and over every time he wants to describe what is happening. But then he shows us that pronouns can come to the rescue, replacing those long, repetitive lists of nouns with a few short words like "I," "he," "she," and "it." Suddenly, the exhaustive string of words that knocked him to the ground is replaced by one short, simple sentence, and the three friends go floating off into the sunset in a balloon. Pronouns save the day![4]

That is a simple part of speech performing its function. We use pronouns and benefit from them, but for the most part we don't even notice them. Ask ten people on the street what a pronoun is, and most will only give you examples of them (he, she, it, we), rather than being able to describe what they do. That's like being asked what a plumber does and responding with the names of three plumbers you know.

For too many people, discovering our life's work is a lot like the casual approach to learning grammar. It's basically accidental. If we get out there and bump into a lot of people who do stuff, maybe we'll find something we like. We let our interests guide us, perhaps following in the footsteps of a parent or relative, or imagining ourselves as part of the latest television drama. Because they are just passing interests, however, we're never sure if we have found a match. But just like the words in a brilliant novel or an essential instruction manual, we all have a function. There is something we are built to do.

Hello, My Name Is . . .

It doesn't take much practice reading before you can pick out nouns and verbs with ease. Imagine if it were just as easy to see what the people around you were built to do. Visualize yourself in a busy place, like a mall or a subway station. You are surrounded by people hurrying here and there. As you look more carefully, however, you see they are all wearing name tags that say, "Hello, my name is," and written in the blank are phrases such as "motivator," "steward," "champion of the helpless," and "technical problem solver." Wouldn't it change the way you interacted with them? Wouldn't there be an extra moment of anticipation as you met each new person, wondering what his or her special identity was? You'd likely watch some of them carefully as they interacted, waiting to see when their hidden skill would shine forth.

Take a minute and try this. Think of the names of three of your friends. Close your eyes and visualize them walking towards you in that crowded mall. They smile and greet you and approach to talk. As they get close, you can see their bright red "Hello, My Name Is . . ." name tags. What do they say? How do they make you feel when you are with them?

Okay, now look down at your own name tag. What is written there?

This is one of our deepest questions. Who has God created me to be? What is the gift that I'm supposed to bring into the world?

3

We all want to make sure we spend our time doing what we were built to do.

When I visualize the name tags for three of my good friends I see:

System Builder

Pursuer of God's Heart

Faithful Steward

God has built people with an incredible variety of functions. Imagine for a moment what the people wearing these name tags would be like.

Customer Service Rock Star

One-woman Welcoming Committee

Make Others Feel Safe

Idea Guy

Can Always Find a Deal

Prayer Warrior

Never Met a Stranger

Champion of the Weak

Your Personal Cheerleader

Show God's Generosity

I Make Everything More Fun

Fearless Inventor

We are all searching for the name on our name tags. We want to know who God created us to be. People think they want power, wealth, influence, or fame, but when they have these things they do not satisfy. Then it becomes clear that what they really want is meaning, reason, and an answer to the question "Why?" What people really need is to know their Function.

Function is the intention for which something was brought into existence. We sense a need for beauty, truth, or comfort, and we create a work of art, a law that protects others, or a wraparound couch. We do not design or build things at random, but

What magic formula did *Schoolhouse Rock* use that made it so easy to remember? Tom Yohe, one of the show's creators, explained, "It was entertaining, and the three minutes were over before the kids knew they were being educated. And of course the repetitions!" *Schoolhouse Rock* was born when an advertising executive realized that his son could remember the lyrics to dozens of songs but struggled with remembering his multiplication tables. Even though *Schoolhouse Rock* went off the air in 1985, my generation has continued to pass our love of it on to our own kids. When I speak to student groups, I only have to sing a few words from a song like "Conjunction Junction," and the students join right in.[5] Just like the repetition in the songs helped viewers remember the function of the words, so using our functions helps us to strengthen and clarify what we were built to do.

full of intention, made to be useful and to serve. We create for a purpose, and so does God.

God has given you a Function—a special gift, a reason for being, a little piece of God's glory to bring into the world. It may not be as obvious as a name tag, but it will show up clearly when you start looking, and it is likely visible to others in some way now.

You have a choice. Some people remain largely ignorant of their Function, disbelieving in God or in God's special design for each person, or so caught up in living that they never look. Others have an inkling of what their gift is but choose to reject it and redirect their energies toward a path of their own choosing, trying to work around God's design. You can, however, choose to discover and embrace your Function, seeking to live your life from the power and purpose that God offers.

This is the choice I want to make. I want to know who God created me to be, and I want to live from it. If that is your choice as well, I invite you to walk with me through this book, asking God to teach you how to let the Creator's design shine forth in you.

The PIE Principle of Career Planning

Your Function is something you will use in all areas of your life—interacting with your friends, family, and neighbors. The clearest application of knowing your Function, however, is discovering how to use it in your work. This book will help you discover your Function, but it will also guide you to use that knowledge practically by applying it to your career. Good career planning requires a systematic approach. Too many career advising systems rely on just one aspect of the career development process, whether it is interests, personality testing, skills, or values. None of these approaches addresses the complex design that God gave each of us when we were created. Instead, we need to use a well-developed framework that allows us to put all of the pieces of the puzzle together and to test them.

The method I have used successfully with both individual students and my career classes I call the PIE principle. The concept behind PIE was inspired by the work of author Jim Collins in his groundbreaking business book, *Good to Great*, published in the year 2001.

In *Good to Great*, Collins studied why some companies were able to make amazing leaps to business greatness, while other companies that looked very similar from the outside never seemed to make it past "good." Collins's great companies used a disciplined approach to discover where their strengths and opportunities overlapped.

Collins advised companies to look for three things: 1) what they are passionate about, 2) what they can be best in the world at, and 3) what drives their economic engines. The overlap of these three areas created a central concept that should guide the company to greatness.[6]

In career planning, there is a similar set of questions that can help you to understand what you were built to do and what can bring you success and satisfaction. But it has to start with God. God is your original architect. God's design creates the foundation for your purpose, but God offers you the opportunity to build on that foundation with your own interests and creativity. If you do so, you can discover your Function—the work you were built to do.

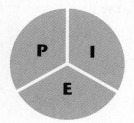

Much like Collins's companies, we'll start with three basic building blocks—three pieces of a pie—we will use to construct a whole picture of your career plan: Purpose (P), Inspiration (I), and Earnings Equation (E).

Your Purpose is the reason you were born. God specially equips each person with the ability to perform a certain role. Working in your Purpose is doing what you are best at.

Your Inspiration is what you love most. It may or may not be something you have natural ability to do, but it is what you never get tired of doing and what most catches your interest.

Your Earnings Equation is a way to package your abilities so that others will pay you to use them. This is critical. Without this element, the other two pieces will not become your primary work.

We are looking for the intersection of these three pieces—the place where what you were born to do and what you love to do becomes what you are paid to do.

Form follows function—that has been misunderstood. Form and function should be one, joined in a spiritual union. —Frank Lloyd Wright[7]

I recently met with a student who was struggling to find the right fit in a career. Her family wanted her to be a doctor, but she was pretty sure that was not a match. After some initial career planning exercises in which she was able to look back on her life, it was clear that she was gifted at communicating, and especially for training, motivating, and persuading people. We put this information into Piece 1.

When I spoke with her about her inspirations and passions, two elements jumped out. First, she loved foreign cultures, especially Asian cultures, and was invigorated by connecting with international people. Second, she was fascinated by art. She loved to draw, read all about art, and collect anime. We listed these insights in Piece 2.

Now came the moment of truth. How could she find her Earnings Equation and pull them all together? I asked her to brainstorm a list of any job she could think of that would allow her to train, motivate, and persuade others and to involve her interests in other cultures and possibly art. It took only a few minutes before she was coming up with all kinds of businesses that would want to hire someone who could sell, market, and train others on their products internationally. She could work in marketing for an international company and stay close to her love of art by designing. Or she could work for a company that dealt in international art, or she could teach Asian art and culture in one of many settings. She couldn't wait to get exploring!

All Three Pieces

One of the biggest pitfalls of career planning is not identifying and developing all three pieces. Think about it. What would happen if one or more pieces were missing from the equation?

Let's say you have fantastic math skills and are great at analyzing things (Purpose). Your parents and teachers convince you that people who are great at math should be accountants because it pays well (Earnings Equation). You enter the field of accounting, but you are not inspired by it. In fact, it drives you crazy. You will either have to get used to doing something you have no interest in or figure out a way to change careers.

Or, let's say you are passionate about music (Inspiration). You love music and know all about it. You are sure you could be part of the next world-famous band (Earnings Equation). There's only one problem—you can't sing or play an instrument. You are working outside of your Purpose.

This one is pretty easy to guess. Let's say you are fantastic at designing creative things with your hands. You are also passionate about recycling, and you decide to make a career out of making trash art. The only problem is that no one seems to want to pay very much for trash art, so you have to get other jobs to support your art as a hobby.

All three pieces of PIE are essential for finding a career where you can be who you are and be successful doing it. You were created with a purpose, and your experiences have shaped your passions. Now it is time to clarify what they are and to discover where you can use them. That is the PIE Principle. As we begin to put the pieces of the PIE together, ask yourself these questions:

1. Who am I, and what skills do I use best?

2. Where would I love to use them?

3. How can I earn a living doing this?

The pieces of the PIE principle—Purpose, Inspiration, and Earnings—interlock to create your Function. This Function is the central concept that should guide the work you do. It will show you how to have maximum impact and career satisfaction. Find your Function, and you will discover what you were built to do.

PURPOSE + INSPIRATION + EARNINGS = FUNCTION

Before we leave this chapter, see if you can identify which pieces of a person's Function are missing in the examples below.

I love animals and have always imagined myself as a veterinarian. I know I could make a good living, but I've heard that veterinary school is even tougher to get into than medical school. When I look at the classes I need to take, it looks like an awful lot of science. Science has usually been my worst subject—all that memorizing. There has to be an easier way!

Missing Piece: _____

I'm a theater nut. I did lot of acting in high school and some in college, but I never finished my degree. I always received terrific feedback, and I just love being on stage. I can't wait to see what new shows are coming out, and I save up every year to make at least one trip to Broadway to see a show. I would love to be a full-time actor. I've had some great community theater parts, but I've been stuck with a couple of part-time jobs to support myself. I think a degree from a well-known school might help me, but it seems like you need to have a big network of contacts to make it in this field.

Missing Piece: _____

I like being a vice president. I have a nice office, a company car, and the respect of my coworkers. My area is sales, and I'm good at it. I know how to build great relationships with clients that keep them coming back as repeat customers. I get to take prospective clients golfing and to sporting events—both of which I enjoy. I'm confident I can keep getting great sales results, but I wish I believed in the product I'm selling. Even though I have all these perks, sometimes it is depressing to think that what we make doesn't seem to make anyone's life better. The thrill of the chase is terrific, but when I look back, will I be satisfied with what I did all these years of my work?

Missing Piece: _____

You are not here merely to make a living. You are here in order to enable the world to live more amply, with greater vision, with a finer spirit of hope and achievement. You are here to enrich the world, and you impoverish yourself if you forget the errand. —Woodrow Wilson[8]

NOTES

1. "Conjunction Junction," *Schoolhouse Rock*, 1973. Music and lyrics by Bob Dorough, sung by Jack Sheldon, designed by Tom Yohe/Bill Peckman, animated by Phil Kimmelman & Associates, produced by Scholastic Rock, Inc.

2. "A Noun Is a Person, Place, or Thing," *Schoolhouse Rock*, 1973, lyrics, music, and performance by Lynn Ahrends; "Unpack Your Adjectives," *Schoolhouse Rock*, 1975, lyrics and music by George R. Newell, performed by Blossom Dearie, 1975, produced by Scholastic Rock, Inc.

3. "Lolly, Lolly, Lolly, Get Your Adverbs Here," *Schoolhouse Rock*, 1974, written and performed by Bob Dorough, produced by Scholastic Rock, Inc.

4. "Rufus Xavier Sarsaparilla," *Schoolhouse Rock*, 1977, written by Bob Dorough and Kathy Mandy, sung by Jack Sheldon, produced by Scholastic Rock, Inc.

5. Michael Miller, "Schoolhouse Rock Did Just That," *Silicon Valley Business Journal*, January 28, 2001.

6. Swarup Bose, review of Jim Collins, *Good to Great: Why Some Companies Make the Leap . . . and Others Don't* (New York: Harper Business, 2001), chap. 5, http://www.sjtvu.com/pw/yanyuyu/e-books/pdf/good%20to%20great.pdf.

7. Frank Lloyd Wright, quote from the George and Eleanor Stockman House website, http://www.stockmanhouse.org/#!flw-quotes/c10ku.

8. Woodrow Wilson, from his speech "Ideals of College," October 25, 1913, www.ordinarypeoplecanwin.com/greatthings.htm.

CHAPTER 2

Help! I Think My Work Is Cursed!

The Meaning, Misery, and Mystery of Work

For we are God's handiwork, created in Christ Jesus to do good works, which God prepared in advance for us to do. —EPHESIANS 2:10

We often miss opportunity because it's dressed in overalls and looks like work. —ANONYMOUS[1]

Lulu the pig had a job to do. There aren't too many things you are well-suited for when you are a 150-pound potbellied pig. You are not likely to win your owner any ribbons for "Best in Show," nor can you help your person stay in shape through exercise. Lulu was not trained as a seeing-eye pig, nor could she bark if intruders came to the door. What Lulu could do was be a faithful companion to her owner.

One day Lulu's Function was put to the test. Her owner had a heart attack and needed medical attention. Lulu sensed something was wrong but did not have a lot of options for responding. Dialing 911 is not easy for those with hooves (dogs have done it!), and CPR was out of the question. So Lulu used the gifts she had been given as a pig to the best of her ability. She squeezed her way through a dog door and went out into the street. When she got there, she got attention like a pig. She lay down in the middle of the street until a passing driver noticed her huge bulk and wondered what was happening. When the driver came out to check on her, Lulu led the person to her owner.[2]

In this true story, Lulu gives us all an example of using everything you have to fulfill a mission. She did not have a lot of skills, but she was a pig with a purpose. Biblical and historical church traditions teach us that the purpose of human beings is to worship God. This is true, but it is a bit like telling Lulu to be a pig, without any kind of individual instructions. We also need to recognize that God has something "prepared in advance" for each of us. Like Lulu, we each have a job to do, and doing this job or performing this role is a big part of how we worship God and bring him glory.

The human creature was made to worship in a very specific way, by interacting with the earth. We are commissioned by God to work and develop the earth in a way that represents God's will and brings Him glory. —J. Richard Middleton[3]

Not Just a Job

The terms "function" and "purpose" are intimately linked. Our Purpose (our reason for being) is realized only in our doing (our Function). As Gerard Manley Hopkins put it, "What I do is me: for that I came."[4]

What you do is your work. To work is nothing more than applying effort to have an effect on something around you. There are two ways we do this in life. The first is to have a job, which is work that creates an economic benefit (though you may sometimes wonder how much economic benefit *you* are getting). Your effort in a job provides a benefit to an organization, and one hopes that organization passes on some of that benefit to you. The government also gets a benefit from your work and passes benefits back to you (and lots of other people, too). If you are self-employed, you skip the middleman (or woman) and create economic benefit

For an alternative way of thinking about the economic benefit you provide when you work, check out "Calculating the Economic Value of Volunteers" at www.handsonnetwork.org/tools/ volunteercalculator. This site will show you the hourly rate it would cost for an agency to replace the specialized work you might do as a volunteer. Say you worked forty hours a week, fifty weeks a year (assuming two weeks' vacation annually). That's two thousand hours. Let's assume you work from age twenty to age sixty-five—a total of forty-five years. At two thousand hours a year, that's ninety thousand hours in your lifetime. Multiply your hourly rate in the volunteer calculator by ninety thousand to get what you economic value would be to a volunteer organization if you volunteered for them for your working life. That's a lot of good!

for yourself. If you are a full-time parent, you provide an economic benefit to the organization that is your family.

Everyone who is capable of producing an economic benefit is expected to do so. A job, of one kind or another, is an inescapable reality of life. And it represents a huge chunk of our time. For many people, however, it is time lost. For some, it is a daily activity that they passively accept in order to have spending money and leisure time on nights and weekends. Bright, talented people show up at their place of work every day, checking their hats at the door with their brains inside them. This is incredibly sad. In my mind that is akin to getting married and having children in order to get a tax break. For others, work is worse. It is more like prison. These folks are not able to check their minds at the door. They know they are in bad work situations but feel helpless to change them.

This is not the case for everyone, however. Some people seem to discover the secret of finding meaning and reward in the work they do. Some of these folks are well-paid, some are not, but they all seem to get an additional, nonmonetary paycheck from their employer that remains invisible to others. These people don't find work burdensome, and many look forward to going to work most days. Oddly enough, this sense of satisfaction is not dependent on the job being easy or prestigious. Some individuals thrive in challenging, even stressful, jobs, and others never receive significant recognition for the work that they do, but they love it anyway. Some great mystery is at work (literally).

The other type of work we do is our Purpose. Your Purpose is the work that you do because it is who you are, rather than because it is your job title. Perhaps you naturally seek to serve the practical needs of others in a specific way. When your church or club organizes meals for someone who is sick, your name comes up to lead the effort. You anticipate that your neighbor will need help shoveling snow off his driveway, and you go to help before shoveling your own. When you plan a trip with a group, you bring the snacks and plan the best places for pit stops. Nobody hired you to do this, but it is work nonetheless. You have a skill in this area that shines forth, often without you even knowing.

Or maybe you are a natural encourager. You call right before someone's big test to cheer him or her on. You notice when people seem discouraged, and you seek ways to help them reenergize. You are constantly slipping your family members notes or inspirational or self-help books they "just have to read." This is work that feels effortless because you are specially equipped to do it. Typically we do not think much about this kind of work that we do; it just comes out as an expression of who we are. In fact, if we choose not to do this natural work, or if we are taught that our particular Purpose is not valuable, we find ourselves frustrated and restless.

During most of our lives, we will do both kinds of work. We will spend countless hours at some kind of job, but what will these hours mean? What should they mean?

Many persons have a wrong idea of what constitutes true happiness. It is not attained through self-gratification but through fidelity to a worthy purpose.
—Helen Keller[5]

Career Planning Paralysis

Some people are wary of using personality assessments to assist in their career decision making. I find these assessments extremely helpful. God has gifted certain people with the ability to see patterns in human creation and to provide a common language for us to communicate about it. Theories are approximations, but they can be enormously useful in helping us to see ourselves accurately, to understand why we feel the way we do, and to make better choices about how to move forward.

One of the most well-known and respected personality theories is the Myers-Briggs™ typology. The Myers-Briggs typology is an incredibly rich theory, with lots of complexity and nuance, but certain pieces of it are accessible, and I have found them valuable for assisting others with career planning.

In particular, I tend to use a small piece of this theory when helping people through what I call career planning paralysis. Most people experience this as a feeling of being stuck in picking a forward path for their careers. I recently met with a student who is three years into his college career and still has not picked a major. He knows he needs to, but he keeps agonizing over the decision. He's developed a list of options, but every time he tries to match his interests with a field or to rank one potential major over another, the picture gets cloudy. He has interests but doesn't feel like he can trust himself to make a good decision.

By contrast, I have also met with established professionals who have the opposite problem. They have been working for years in a field but realize they are in the wrong career. They are eager to make a change and willing to do whatever work I suggest, but they can't quite get their heads around the fact that they could choose careers that are unrelated to their training. They try to imagine other opportunities, but they can't fathom why anyone would hire them for anything except what their college diploma says. A seventh-grade math teacher with this type of paralysis, if asked for a dream list of other possible jobs, would say, "high-school math teacher, elementary-school math teacher, college math professor, middle-school administrator."

When I meet with folks suffering from this type of paralysis, I often share some Myers-Briggs basics. I tell them that the theory postulates that people have two basic functions that comprise their personality. The first is a perceiving function, which describes how they take in information about the world around them. Individuals prefer to take in information either by sensing, which is using their senses to recognize observable facts, or through intuition, which is recognizing the connections between things that are often not clearly visible or making mental leaps to fill in the blanks of a situation.

As I visualize it, the sensing person might go through a checkout line and notice that there are four kinds of gum and one box that needs a refill. There are three people in line, and the cashier is wearing a blue shirt and her name tag says Wanda. The intuitive person might step into the same line and miss all these details but notice that the person in front of him is standing too close to the person in front of her, which is making that person uncomfortable. The cashier's body language suggests that she is exhausted and hates her job, and the last-minute purchases on the checkout aisle all seem to be geared toward male children.

The other central function of the theory is decision making. Once they have collected information about the world around them, individuals use it to make a choice, but they do so one of two ways. Some people prefer to use the thinking function logically to approach decisions. These folks would most likely use a list of pros and cons or compare features between decisions to see which makes the most logical sense. Other individuals choose based on feeling or valuing. These people can appreciate logic, but in the end they make their decision based on a deeply held principle or because it feels right in their gut.[6]

What I find is that younger people who suffer from career planning paralysis tend to struggle because they are not very aware of their preferred decision-making function. Like the young student I mentioned, they've never really thought about whether they typically make decisions based on thinking or feeling. (The Myers-Briggs theory might say that their decision-making function is

17

not well differentiated.) They may think, or hear from parents or friends, that the logical choice is A, but something in their instinct says it is B.

Because they don't have much practice trusting in either their thinking or their feeling to make life-changing choices, they flounder. Often, if they can look back at their lives to see how they made other decisions successfully, they can find the confidence to say, "I'm a good thinker. When I use logic to decide, I tend to make wise choices. What does my logic tell me in this situation?" Or they may say, "This might seem like the logical choice, but if I don't believe it is the right choice, I'm likely to be sorry."

Older career planners, like our friend the math teacher, have had a lot more practice using their decision-making function. In fact, they may be so used to deciding to use their strength that it overpowers their ability to perceive correctly. Before they have had the chance to examine all the evidence about which of their skills match which job descriptions (sensing) or brainstorm creative possibilities of new directions (intuition), their decision-making functions have already taken over and decided that they won't find a fit. In this situation, it is essential that these individuals look back to remind themselves that they are more than their jobs, and that at one point they probably had other interests and skills that they may be able to dust off and use again in a new way.

Both types of paralysis—deciding and perceiving—can make it very difficult to construct any effective career plan, so paralyzed people stay stuck. They don't have the right tools to help them fully develop their career planning muscles. They can take every free Internet quiz and sit in career counseling sessions, but the information doesn't penetrate. It doesn't go deep enough to uproot the doubt we all have about what we are supposed to be doing.

Seriously, if we struggle that much with figuring out what it is we were built to do, do we really believe that a five-minute Internet quiz or a quick conversation with a complete stranger is going to hand us the purpose behind our life's work? No, we don't. At some level, we all know that we need to go to a much deeper source. We need to hear from a much greater authority

How do you make decisions? While researching decision-making styles, I came across this simple exercise on a WikiHow page that I think is a good example of trying to reconcile thinking and feeling decision-making approaches.

At the center top of a piece of paper, write down the change you are considering (e.g., change jobs). To the left, create a column where you list the positive things you think will happen by making the change. To the right, list the negative things you anticipate could happen. To the far left, create another column and write down a rating of 1 to 10 beside each of the positive events to indicate how much of a positive change it would be. To the far right, create another column and write down a rating, this time negative 1 to negative 10, of how significant the effect would be for each negative event.

Add up the two columns, and then add the two scores together. Is the result positive or negative? How positive or negative is it? This is the thinking portion of your decision making. To engage your feeling function, you now ask yourself whether your gut agrees this is right. If your scores and your gut feeling both clearly agree, you can make a pretty confident decision. If they disagree, do some research to see if any of the negatives could be reduced or the positives increased with more time or a change in factors that you control. If you come to the point where your gut and your numbers agree, that is great. If not, revisit this decision in the future when factors may have changed.[7]

who we are and what our work really means, and then we need to see the evidence in our own lives.

There's Always a Wise Guy

The Bible has a lot to say about our work. In particular, I've come to appreciate the wisdom of the book of Ecclesiastes. On the surface, some portions are a bit depressing, as the author labels much of life "meaningless, a chasing after the wind." But I don't think the Teacher's point is to depress us, but rather to remind us that so little of what we spend our days striving for will have any eternal value. We need this reminder of what is real and lasts, and what does not. Every time I read Ecclesiastes, I am challenged to reassess my priorities.

So what does the author say about work? In Ecclesiastes 2, the Teacher criticizes working for rewards and tears apart the idea of building any kind of material legacy, stating that it is meaningless for us to toil only to hand our goods over to someone else when we die. Later in the chapter, however, the Teacher strikes a different chord about work as one of the simple joys of life: "A person can do nothing better than to eat and drink and find satisfaction in their own toil. This too, I see is from the hand of God, for without him, who can eat or find enjoyment? To the person who pleases him, God gives wisdom, knowledge and happiness" (Ecclesiastes 2:24-26).

Later, in Ecclesiastes 3, the Teacher says again: "I know that there is nothing better for people than to be happy and to do good while they live. That each of them may eat and drink, and find satisfaction in all their toil—this is the gift of God" (Ecclesiastes 3:12-13).

In both passages, the author points to satisfaction as the reason for and ultimate goal of work. You might be surprised by this, and some readers would contest it, pointing to the curse on work in Genesis 3. But while our work is certainly plagued by hard toil, and at times futility, we see that work existed before the curse of sin. Human beings were given a Function in the garden— to be its stewards—and both Adam and Eve were charged with populating the world and ruling over it. Their work assignment was pre-Fall. While work can be difficult, it was intended to bring satisfaction, too.

You Are Equipped

But how can we find satisfaction in "all our toil"? What allows us to find meaning in what we do and to move beyond the curse into something that feels more like a reward than a punishment? The key is to narrow the gap between the two types of work that we do—the economic and the functional. If you want to discover a sense of satisfaction in what you do, find your Function and learn to use it with excellence. Then follow that Function to make a living.

Mark Twain once said, "The secret of success is making your vocation your vacation."[8] While I have yet to find anyone who has experienced every day of work as a vacation, Twain was onto something. The satisfaction in our toil comes from being engaged in something meaningful, something in which we can make a noticeable impact, and something we perceive as being a particular fit for us. We want to know that we are not working for the sake of work or just to put bread on the table, but because we are needed and effective. This sense comes from knowing that we are doing what we were designed to do by a God who has equipped us for that purpose.

One of my favorite advertisements of all time was a magazine ad for Swiss Army knives. It showed an open palm holding one of the company's signature knives, with the many compact tools partly showing. The caption read, "Equipped: Just like you."

My first thought was, "Yeah, right." But then I realized that it was right. That is not always what we see when we look in the mirror, but that is how God sees us. We see our faults and our fears, and our past mistakes loom large in our view. God sees our potential and our design. As Ephesians 2:10 says, "For we are God's handiwork, created in Christ Jesus to do good works, which God prepared in advance for us to do."

God has done the equipping. God has given us a Function that our heart wants to perform, and we have the opportunity to seek out situations where that skill is needed. Like the Swiss Army knife, we've been built with tools that spring forward when we have the chance to be put to use.

God built us with a specific Purpose, but that does not mean we are suited for only one perfect job. On the contrary, our special

I find looking at the various types of Swiss Army tools fascinating. I love how each type is designed with a specific person in mind and contains all the gadgets necessary to do a certain kind of job. If you look at the swissarmy.com website, you'll see that the different types of tools have names like Handyman, Tinker, Craftsman, Mechanic, Picnic Set, Caddy, Climber, and Cyber Tool. I think of this as an excellent illustration of how we are designed as well. Just like the name tags from chapter 1, our design name indicates what tools we come equipped with to do the job we are built to do.

An illuminating exercise is to design a Swiss Army knife that represents you. Take a sheet of paper and draw the basic Swiss Army knife shape. Now think about what you feel are your strongest skills. What tasks do others compliment you on or do you do and feel especially effective? Pick a symbol for this skill and try to draw it coming out of the knife handle. If you draw worse than a kindergartener (don't include this as one of your skills!), draw the words coming out of the handle. Now think about the work you are currently doing or work you are planning to do. Draw a second knife handle and sketch in the symbols for the skills needed for that work. How many tools do they have in common? Are you a Caddy with a Tinker's tools? Having the right tools is one of the most important factors for success in doing any job.

equipping can be a match for multiple jobs in a variety of settings. I believe that God wants to lead us to the places where our special Purpose is the most needed and can have the most influence. Often God will guide us to jobs that help us to fine-tune our Purpose, preparing us for more effective work in the future. Like a master craftsman, God arranges to have the right tools in place for the work that needs to be done.

This built-in Purpose seems strangely mysterious, primarily because over the decades we have become distanced from the rest of

God's creation. We view ourselves as separate from the rest of the ordered world, but if we look around, we will see the incredible purposefulness with which God creates. For example, instead of viewing the moon as something pretty to look at during the night, we also know that the pull of the moon causes the tides of the sea and keeps the oceans from stagnating and killing animal and plant life. We may see insects as a nuisance, forgetting they are important pollinators for plants. Trees consume carbon dioxide and produce oxygen, which is consumed by animals that produce carbon dioxide. We are surrounded by a beautiful, intricate, purposeful design.

When we see that everything around us has been given a specific Function, we will not be surprised to find one in ourselves. Knowing we are designed with a Purpose can feel a little threatening if we do not fully trust that God knows what he is doing. Many of us have been told all our lives, "You can be anything you want to be." This may be true (with some logical exceptions) and is a wonderful encouragement for hard work and perseverance, but many times we have come to view this "right to have options" as the highest good in the universe. We would rather keep our options, which we feel are under our control, than to accept God's special gifting if it means limiting ourselves.

This is part of why we struggle so much with balancing our lives. I find it difficult to say no to many of the requests I get and the many things that bombard me. Part of it is that I do not like to disappoint people, but part of it is that I want to keep my options. I am afraid I might be missing out on something. If we could see our Function more clearly and really believed that fulfilling it was God's best for us, saying no would be easy. We would tell others, "That's not what I do best," or "That's not the role God has given me." We would spend more time doing what we were designed to do and less time fouling up other people's things and hitting ourselves on the thumbs with hammers.

Stop for a minute right now and think about a few things that you do on a regular basis that meet this description:

1. Although I might feel like I should do this, I'm not required to by a job description or an ethical mandate.

2. I am not well-equipped for this. This is not one of my strong skills.

3. I really dislike doing this; the only reason I do it is that I feel like I should.

Now ask yourself why you should do this. Answers like, "Because I don't want to hurt someone's feelings," "If I don't do it, who will?" or "Because someone might think less of me" do not count as valid reasons. If you cannot come up with a compelling reason to do something that meets these criteria, you should add this activity to your Not to Do List (NTDL). Eliminating these things is not laziness or selfishness. Your NTDL allows you to spend more time doing what you, and maybe only you, can do.

Function matters. Without it, our working lives are just a transaction—money paid for services rendered. With it, we are living from who we are. Because of Function, we can find satisfaction in our toil. With it, we show the glory of God resonating forth in our everyday work.

Teddy Roosevelt said, "Far and away the best prize that life has to offer is the chance to work hard at work worth doing."[9] As you find what it is that God built you to do and look for opportunities to do it, you can find joy in even very challenging work. You will sense that you were born to do it. You will discover that God has already given you the tools to do it with excellence, reflecting a small fragment of our Creator's glory.

I hope you do care about finding your Function, and that you are willing to do a bit of digging and exploration to discover it. If so, what you uncover can guide and direct your steps at the career crossroads of life.

Just as in any good story, the best place for us to begin is the beginning, so let's look back and see if we can find some clues that will help you in your Function finding.

NOTES

1. Anonymous. This quote was first attributed to Henry Dodd but has also been attributed to others, including Thomas A. Edison. http://quoteinvestigator .com/2012/08/13/overalls-work/.

2. Michael A. Fuoco, "Lulu the Heroic Pig Now Known Worldwide," *Pittsburgh Post-Gazette*, April 9, 2002, http://old.post-gazette.com/neigh_ west/20020409lulu0409p1.asp.

3. J. Richard Middleton, "The Sacred Call to Study," *The Ivy League Christian Observer*, winter 2013, 14.

4. Gerard Manley Hopkins, "As Kingfishers Catch Fire," or untitled, undated, c. 1877, www.gerardmanleyhopkins.org/lectures_2004/As_Kingfishers_ analysis.html.

5. Helen Keller, from *Real Simple* online, Daily Thought, www.realsimple .com/magazine-more/inside-website/daily-thought/happiness-000000000089 53/page20.html.

6. Isabel Briggs Myers, Mary H. McCaulley, Naomi L. Quenk, and Allen L. Hammer, *MBTI Manual: A Guide to the Development and Use of the Myers-Briggs Type Indicator*, 3rd ed. (Mountain View, CA: CPP, 2009), 22–25.

7. "How to Make Tough Decisions for Yourself," WikiHow, www.wikihow .com/Make-Tough-Decisions-for-Yourself.

8. Mark Twain, quoted by Michael McKinney, "Mark Twain on Leadership," *Leadership* blog, April 21, 2010, www.leadershipnow.com/leading blog/2010/04/mark_twain_on_leadership.html.

9. Theodore Roosevelt, "A Square Deal," speech to farmers at the New York State Agricultural Association, Syracuse, NY, September 7, 1903, www .memorablequotations.com/SquareDeal.htm.

CHAPTER 3

Misbehaving on Purpose

Answering the "What?" Question

The glorious masterpiece of man is to live to purpose; all other things: to reign, to lay up treasure, to build, are but little appendices and props. —MICHEL DE MONTAIGNE[1]

The purposes of a person's heart are deep waters, but one who has insight draws them out. —PROVERBS 20:5

I was in second grade, in Mrs. French's class, when I brought home my first C. My parents were shocked. I was one of those kids who loved learning. My parents tell stories of coming into my room and finding me surrounded by piles of books, sitting like a dragon on a clutch of treasure. They would turn off my lights and come back twenty minutes later to find me reading by flashlight under the covers. And I enjoyed school. I had friends and liked my teachers. So why the low grade? And of all things, it was in behavior.

I couldn't explain it. I felt like things were going well in school. My parents made an appointment to see my teacher right away. As they explained it to me, she said, "Aaron is doing well academically, but he can be a little disruptive in class." My mother asked whether I was acting out or being disrespectful. My teacher said, "Not exactly. His problem is talking to others. You see, he usually finishes his work fairly quickly, but then instead of staying at his desk, he goes around the room helping other kids do theirs. He cheers them on and tries to get them to go faster. I appreciate his spirit, but I need the other students to work through it on their own." As you can tell, I haven't changed much!

I got into trouble later that year for another similar teaching moment. I was in the bathroom when a classmate of mine came in. I guess we were both too young to know that guys don't talk in bathrooms, because we somehow got into a big discussion about karate techniques we had seen on television. There was one particular move he didn't seem to understand. I figured I'd better show him, so we acted out some elementary school version of *The Matrix*. My flying kick technique must have been better than I thought, because the next thing I knew I was in the principal's office explaining why I was using the boys' restroom as a dojo.

I wasn't a bad kid, but when I did misbehave, the story was always the same—understanding. Either I did not understand something or I was trying to help someone else understand something. "You were always like that," my mom once told me. "As long as I could explain something to you so that you could understand it, you were fine, but if not—boy, were you stubborn!"

So here is at least one time where behaving badly can work for you. We often spend those early childhood and school years learning to conform. We discover how to live within the bounds of what others expect of us. That special set of gifts that God has given you, however, is not going to fit in naturally with the norm. It is going to squeeze out somewhere. For better or worse, by looking back at your past, the easiest place to perceive that unique gift is usually where you were coloring outside the lines. If you can find a theme in the times you caused the most mischief, you are probably not far from the Purpose you were trying (unsuccessfully) to express.

Colonel Mustard, in the Dining Room, with the Candlestick

Let's face it, most of us do not change all that much between the ages of two and twenty-five. A few decades ago, the debate

Ten Bad Childhood Behaviors
That Can Work to Your Advantage

Recognize any of these behaviors? What looks like a weakness can be developed into a natural strength.

CHILDHOOD TRAIT	POTENTIAL POSITIVE
Bossy	Leadership potential
Picky	Ability to discover what others don't see
Chatterbox	Great communicator
Manipulative	Inspiring
Cuts corners	Efficient
Clown	Creatively identifies opportunities
Hypercompetitive	Enterprising
Clingy	Sensitive to the needs of others
Stubborn	Strong core values
Rough/Physical	Craftsmanship abilities

between nature and nurture was at the forefront of science. But ask parents of multiple children, and they will tell you that you never know what flavor you'll get wrapped up in that swaddling blanket. Sure, as we grow we add skills and learn to better control the way we are perceived, but kids are born different from each other. Most children born into the same family environment— even twins—often develop very different personalities from an early age. How amazing that God put a divine fingerprint on each individual life in a unique way. It is at this beginning of your story you should begin to look for the clues God has left for you.

I did survive elementary school without causing my parents too much further embarrassment. In fact, there were some positive aspects of my "need for understanding gene," as well. Besides the fact that I wrote great book reports, I began to develop an ability to connect well with people and bridge gaps in understanding.

Around the same time as the *Matrix* incident, my parents began to see me flex these understanding muscles.

When I was eight, my family took a trip to Florida. As we boarded the plane, we noticed that three of our seats were together and one was several rows ahead. My parents assumed that one of them would sit up front, but I convinced them that I could handle the solo seat. I sat down next to a Cuban-American gentleman and introduced myself. By the time we got off the plane in Florida, he had taught me to count to one hundred in Spanish, and I had memorized a dozen other words as well. Not a typical plane flight for an eight-year-old.

So was this a random occurrence or a clue? The only way to know whether an event like this is pointing to your Purpose is to look for evidence of a sustained pattern in your life. Ask yourself, "Can I connect the dots between the skill I am using (or the reason I keep getting into trouble) and a string of other events in my life before and since?" If the answer is yes, ask yourself, "Is this something that God could get glory from if I use it correctly?" Match the fingerprints, and you will find the author.

The pattern of promoting understanding continued for me. In high school I was friends with all the exchange students. I could sense that they had all this amazing, bottled-up potential in there that others couldn't see because of the cultural barrier. I was drawn to them, and I did everything I could to help them make connections and thrive in their new environment. Others noticed this desire to connect, too. One year I was chosen as the only student in my class to attend a leadership program. A teacher told me that it wasn't because I was the smartest or the most talented, but because several teachers had noticed the way that I had reached out to the exchange students and helped them to be successful. (Looking back, that is one of the strangest compliments I have ever received!)

Connecting with exchange students inspired me to continue studying languages and learn all I could about other countries. Later I became an exchange student myself and loved feeling like an ambassador. I spent a year in South America and absorbed everything I could. Want to take tango lessons? Yes! Are you interested in being interviewed by the local radio station? Sure! Want to go cheese shopping in the next town? Of course! Connect, learn, mentor. Grow, grow, grow.

Decades later, none of that has changed. I now drive people at my office crazy by making them take personality quizzes so that they can learn to work together better, and I am usually dabbling with two or three travel ideas and trying to learn a couple of foreign languages (not always successfully) at any given time. Just recently I found myself trying to help international students on my campus network to find on-campus jobs. I don't do it because it is part of my job description; I do it because it is who I am.

This is why feedback from those who know us well is critical. Ask your parents. What was it about you that surprised them? Each of us had some way in which we seemed out of step with other children our age. Some kids pick out minute differences that no one else seems to notice. Others can build something out of anything. Some of us are born leaders, organizing other kids at game time and driving our parents crazy because we know a better way to do everything.

My son has been captivated by sounds since he was young. He learned early to say his letters, and random words like "rags" would send him into fits of laughter because of their unusual sound. He has always loved inventing languages and strange names of characters. At the age of ten, he had built whole worlds for his characters, complete with important-sounding battles and dynasties of oddly named kings that go back hundreds of years. Like any parent, I wonder why God gave him this particular gift. What will he do with it? That part of his personality has not changed since he was two.

My daughter, by contrast, is a problem solver. She excels at all kinds of crafts and hands-on activities, she aces word scrambles, and she has this surprising knack for coming up with outside-the-box solutions for everyday problems. The rest of the family will be puzzled by a challenge, and she will say, "Wouldn't it be great if someone invented a. . . . That would take care of this problem."

Top Ten Reasons to Live in Another Culture

Not everyone enjoys international cultures and travel the way that I do, but I would still recommend that everyone have some type of real intercultural experience. If you can't live in another country for a while, take a significant trip where you can serve in an international setting, volunteer for an organization that serves a different cultural group in your area, or give serious effort to language study. It may feel a little awkward at first, but consider the benefits:

10. You will have the opportunity to comprehend the world from a different perspective. This removes some assumptions that we all live with every day but don't realize.

9. Gaining experience with another language will give you a window into a new world you have not explored, and it will help you understand your own language better. I have learned more about English grammar from studying other languages than I ever did in English class.

8. Intercultural experience and foreign language ability are marketable skills for your résumé.

7. You are likely to have a chance to try some fantastic food you never knew existed.

6. Your understanding and compassion for people different from you will grow.

5. It will make you a bit bolder and more comfortable in new environments.

4. You will realize that the American concept of time, as something we are always chasing and can never get enough of, is not the only way to live.

3. You will likely make friends and memories you will cherish for life.

2. It makes a great topic of conversation, whether you are at a dinner party, on a date, or in a job interview.

1. You will never see yourself the same way again.

Recently she was mourning the loss of a swing set, which she and her brother had outgrown. When I challenged her to think about what new opportunities could come from this, she brought out a page-long list of appropriate yard toys and equipment she recommended—problem solved.

We should not be surprised by these little glimpses of our Function peeking through at an early age. God wants you to understand your design and Purpose. If you seek clues, you will find them, because God left them there to be found.

In *Finding God Where You Least Expect Him*, author John Fischer describes a life of following God as a great game of hide and seek.

> Ever notice that with a small child something hidden is always more intriguing than something found? In spite of what they say, the two birds in the bush are far more interesting than the one in the hand. It's a little like that with God. He lures us into the mystery. His concealment is an invitation to find out. And like a good father, at the right time, he brings what was hidden out into full view. He does not always frustrate us. It's the way it has always been: God hides; we seek.[2]

One of the glimpses God gives is that little bit of unique design put in each of us. Truly here is evidence of how intimately our Creator knows us, and how much God values us to give us a special role to play. But the message is not just for us. The fingerprint that God has left on our lives is also a clue to others—a tiny peek at God's glory that inspires others to seek and find.

Recognizing Yourself

A couple of years ago, my wife signed up to be a volunteer for the television show *Extreme Makeover Home Edition* when it rebuilt a home in our area. The show's star, Ty Pennington, has done a huge amount of good by helping families in need get the homes of their dreams. Ty has a larger-than-life personality, and he is obviously passionate about what he's doing. He's found a way to make a great living (be a television star) doing what he has been

Create Your Own Personality Test

There are hundreds of personality quizzes in circulation, but you can get some of the same insights into your personality and passions by creating your own personality test. There's no science here, but these activities are a fun warm-up for the work we'll do in a few pages.

1. If you have a computer, go to your Internet browser and write down the list of all the "favorites" links you have saved. Now cross out anything that you need only for your work or family responsibilities. What is left? Write a one or two-sentence description of yourself based only on these links. For example, mine might say, "Aaron is clearly fascinated with personality quizzes, career development, and topics of history and culture. He likes foreign languages (but can't seem to decide which one to study), inspirational Christian blogs, education reform, and writing." To some degree, you are what you read!

2. Select three friends and give each one a sheet of paper. Ask them each to write down the three words or phrases they think best describe you. Compile the answers. This is the personality you project to the outside world. Does it describe how you experience your personality? If not, compare how you envision yourself with how others perceive you. Write a brief description about yourself, crafting one paragraph from the feedback you received and one paragraph from how you perceive yourself. If you are brave enough, share this with your friends. You'll be amazed by what you learn.

specially gifted to do. Like many of us, his Function materialized early too. As *The Encyclopedia of World Biography* describes:

As a child, Pennington learned woodworking from his father. He would tear apart furniture and turn them into toys. His mother sent him outside to build something that he could then destroy. He gathered up the neighborhood kids, negotiated pay at three comic books per hour, borrowed tools from their parents, and then constructed a three-story tree house.³

I wish that someone had told me to look for fingerprints like these when I was a teen or a college student trying to figure out what to do with my life. The temptation to solve life's riddles by the world's wisdom is really strong at that age. We get a lot of pressure and conflicting messages about what success is and what is expected of us. Ecclesiastes 11:9 counsels,

> You who are young, be happy while you are young,
>   and let your heart give you joy in the days of your youth.
> Follow the ways of your heart
>   and whatever your eyes see.

It is often at this age that we intentionally *stop* following our hearts and try to follow our heads. But it is upon our hearts that God has signed the divine name. As Ecclesiastes 3:11 states, "[God] has also set eternity in the human heart; yet no one can fathom what God has done from beginning to end." Instead of following the clues God has left for us about our Function, money, success, and responsibility often become our guides. There is a reason that the teacher of Ecclesiastes writes to the young. An honest read through that book might help us all at that age.

As I entered the work world, and as I grew in my faith, the Lord was merciful in teaching me more about the Function instilled in me, but it took me time to recognize it. God gave me clues, often through the people around me, but I had not been taught to look for them. God has given you clues as well. Have you seen them?

> *The purpose of life is to contribute in some way to making things better.* —Robert F. Kennedy⁴

Filling Big Shoes

After you ask what skills you have been using since you were very young, ask yourself who has inspired you. Who were the

> ## The Power of Influence
>
> Take a minute to think about someone who has inspired and influenced you. What did they give you that was so valuable? Write the answers to these questions:
>
> 1. If I wrote a thank-you note to this person, what would it say?
> 2. If I could have lunch with this person today, what would I most want to talk about with him or her?
> 3. In what ways would I want my life to match this person's experience? In what ways do I hope it does not?

people in your life who most influenced its direction? You may have spent lots of time with them if they were relatives or friends, but that is not a prerequisite. What mattered was that rubbing shoulders with someone with similar gifts illuminated what was written on your own heart.

Your influencers might not have been people you have met. They could be historical figures whose examples consistently inspired you to greatness, such as Thomas Edison, Julia Child, Jackie Robinson, Amelia Earhart, Oprah, or Walt Disney. They might not even be real people. Many individuals have been greatly influenced by the characters in books and movies who lived out their values in a clear way, such as Robin Hood (social justice), Lucy from *The Lion, the Witch, and the Wardrobe* (bravery), Kermit the Frog (following your dream), or Indiana Jones (heroism and adventure). Sometimes these characters provide a clearer image of the kinds of people we know we were created to be. The litmus test for influencers is whether or not that person's example compelled you out and up into a bigger sense of who you are. Did you see in them your own gifts fully grown?

Once you identify who your influencers were, ask why. What was it about them that created a natural sense of connection? When they inspired you, were they working in their economic work (paid job) or their functional work (their natural gifts)? Can you see yourself working in that same field or with those same skills? Imagine yourself in their shoes. How do you think those shoes would fit?

Dis-covering Purpose

A. W. Tozer's *The Pursuit of God* is one of my favorites. Seldom has any writer better captured what it means to experience knowing God and the way it changes lives. One day as I was rereading *Pursuit*, I stumbled at one sentence that did not seem right. It talked about God "discovering" himself to us. I thought, "That's not correct; it is the person looking who discovers something. How can God discover himself?" By the third reading, I realized where the word *discover* must have come from: dis-cover. In other words, it was not the way we often use the word to mean searching out and planting a flag on some distant land. *Discover* here meant to take away the covering or the veil that keeps us from seeing what is true.[5] This meaning is absolutely accurate for the work we are doing in understanding Purpose.

In our search for Purpose, we are not creating or shaping our gifts. We are not the first to learn who we are or what we were meant to do, as if we are stepping foot on an uncharted land. We are pulling back the curtain to see what God has already put there. The Lord is well aware of what we will find and eager for us to find it, but our Purpose has been veiled by the dust and dirt of our years of living.

Often, we lose clarity about that Purpose because we think we are insignificant or that our lives do not make a difference on a grand scale. I like how John Eldredge describes it:

> "I'd love to be William Wallace [the hero of *Braveheart*], leading the charge with a big sword in my hand," sighed a friend. "But I feel like I'm the guy back there in the fourth row with a hoe." That's a lie of the Enemy—that your place is really insignificant, that you aren't armed for it anyway. In your life you *are* William Wallace—who else could be? . . . If you leave your place in the line, it will remain empty. No one else can be who you are meant to be.[6]

Sometimes our family and friends also make it more difficult for us to find our Purpose. I have seen this often as I work with students. Sometimes younger children are expected to follow in their older siblings' footsteps ("If only you were more like your older sister!") and live up to their legacy. You may have been born into a family where your Purpose is not valued. Maybe that early evidence of God's fingerprints that you demonstrated as a child was treated as a negative trait.

What expectations did you feel from your family when you were growing up? How do you think they shaped you? Do you still feel them now? To what extent do you think those expectations were a good fit with your personality?

Some parents are determined that their children will follow them into the family business or a socially acceptable field. Others try to make up for the guidance they never received by giving their children more guidance than those kids can handle. In some families it is clear that one child's gifts are valued more than another's. Unfortunately, this process of discovering can sometimes be more like digging, unearthing your Purpose from under layers of other people's junk. That is where the Holy Spirit becomes essential.

Illumination

It is the Spirit who truly uncovers our design by coming to live in the heart of each believer. In our exploration we may brush away some dust, but it is the Holy Spirit who reveals the fingerprints and artifacts—a trail of clues in our experiences—that are there for us to find.

Most of us (myself included) vastly underestimate the potential power of the Holy Spirit in our lives. We are so used to relying on our own power and wisdom, as if God had left us completely alone and naked in the world. When I have a problem, where do I go first? I look it up on the Internet. If I can't find it there, I look for a book or call a friend or turn on the television. Why is it that asking the Holy Spirit to work in the situation comes in around option number 10? But when we receive Christ, God put the Holy Spirit right inside us, and the Spirit's purpose and function is to give us wisdom and counsel. As *The Message*, Eugene Peterson's translation of the Bible in contemporary language, puts it: "But when the Friend comes, the Spirit of Truth, he will take you by the hand and guide you into all the truth there is. . . . He will honor me: he will take from me and deliver it to you" (John 16:12-15). I once heard a Bible professor share an analogy to illustrate this point:

> Once there was a man who wanted to clear the trees from a field so that he could plant it. Day after day he took his ax to the field to cut trees. It was long, tiring work, and he made slow progress.
>
> One day a neighbor came to visit him. When he saw how big the field was, and how little had been cleared, he said, "Friend, you need to go down to the hardware store and get one of those fancy new chainsaws. You'll be able to take those trees down in no time."
>
> The man resisted the idea initially, but after a few more days of slogging away in the sun, he decided it was worth a try. So he left for the hardware store.
>
> He told the manager about his problem, and the manager said, "You've come to the right place. Take this chainsaw here. I guarantee you that if you use this you will clear that field in less than a quarter of the time it would take you to do it by hand."
>
> So the man bought the chainsaw and set off for home, ready to conquer the field.
>
> The next day, when the hardware store manager came in to open the shop, the man was waiting at the door with his chainsaw. His hair was a mess, he had cuts and bruises all over him, and he was fuming.
>
> "You sold me this piece of junk, and it doesn't work. You told me I would clear the field in one quarter of the time, but I worked all yesterday and hardly cut down a tree. I want my money back, and I want an apology!"
>
> "Wow," said the manager. "I can't believe it. We've never had a problem with these. People usually love them. You are sure it doesn't work?"
>
> "Not at all! It would barely cut."
>
> "Okay, let me take a look." The store manager took the chainsaw, flipped the on switch, pulled the cord, and the chainsaw roared to life.
>
> "Yikes!" yelled the man. "What is that? Turn off that awful noise!"

And so it is with us. We've been given the Holy Spirit to work in us in power, and we're trying to make the Spirit work in our old way of doing things. One of the Holy Spirit's jobs in our lives is to be what I think of as the Great Illuminator. We can go forward, confidently knowing that the Spirit's power working within us will reveal who we are and who we were intended to be.

Should we choose to accept it, this uncovering of our Purpose is one of the great missions and potential joys of our lives. It is a gift from God, but as we open the gift, we find another wrapped inside, and another, and another. If we are willing, God shows us where to apply these gifts at different stages of our lives. The gift of Purpose is the first and most essential building block of finding your life's work. Before you know what you should do, you have to know who you are and how you are equipped.

Most of us would prefer to be able to take a quick, multiple-choice quiz and have our Purpose pop out, but that is not how God designed it. The Lord knows that much of the value of finding your Purpose is in the process, so discovering your Purpose requires some exploration work. But starting with the right questions will help, and that is what the Purpose Finder Assessment (chapter 5) in this book is built to do. First, however, let's take a look at how this whole Purpose thing got started.

NOTES

1. Michel de Montaigne, *Essays of Montaigne*, 1877, translated by Charles Cotton, edited by William Carew Hazlitt, produced by David Widger, Project Gutenberg, www.gutenberg.org/files/3600/3600-h/3600-h.htm.

2. John Fischer, *Finding God Where You Least Expect Him* (Eugene, OR: Harvest House, 2003), 43.

3. Ashyia N. Henderson, "Ty Pennington," *Encyclopedia of World Biography*, www.notablebiographies.com/newsmakers2/2005-La-Pr/Pennington-Ty.html #ixzz1ad5GYT6s.

4. Goodreads.com, www.goodreads.com/author/quotes/98221.Robert_F_Kennedy.

5. A. W. Tozer, *The Pursuit of God* (Harrisburg, PA: Christian Publications, 1948), 65.

6. John Eldredge, *Wild at Heart* (Nashville: Thomas Nelson, 2001), 142.

CHAPTER 4

It Is All God's Fault
Following a Purpose-full God

And we know that in all things God works for the good of those
who love him, who have been called according to his purpose.
—ROMANS 8:28

Does not the potter have the right to make out of the same lump
of clay some pottery for special purposes and some for common use?
—ROMANS 9:21

A Painting Parable

The world's most renowned artist had just completed his latest
masterwork. It began as a seed in his mind and became a vision of
a painting like nothing anyone had ever seen. He labored in secret
at first, forming the outline, testing the hues he would use, and
always seeking to capture his own heart and will on the canvas.
As the time approached for his masterpiece to be revealed, he allowed the secret to leak, and the whole art community was abuzz
in anticipation of the reveal.

When the day finally came, the artist spared no expense to
heighten the drama or underscore the importance of his creation.
He built an entire gallery just for the new painting, full of lesser
works and a chronicle of the project. He wanted all the world to
know that what they were seeing had never been created before.

When the moment came and the curtain was thrown back
from the canvas, every eye widened in awe and every mouth was
struck silent in wonder. Not only was the painting beautiful and

intricate beyond belief, but also the artist had done what no other had dreamed. He had created a masterwork with a will of its own. Indeed, as the audience stood in rapt attention, the artist conversed with his painting, and the canvas responded.

For weeks, no one could speak of anything else but the painting into which the artist had painted a bit of his own soul. The artist himself lived in joy and wonder in those weeks, spending hours in the company of his painting, glorying in the interaction between creator and work that shared the same heart. The painting felt the glow of admiration from every visitor and reveled in the company of its creator, knowing it was the artist's greatest achievement.

Alas, however, this bliss did not last. The painting did not remain content. One day it asked itself, "Why should I be the work and not the master? Why can I not choose some other purpose for myself?"

So the masterpiece ripped itself from its canvas and stole out of the gallery. It looked into the wide world and thought, "I am free! Now what do I want to be?" It went out into the streets and tried to speak to everyone it met. But strangely, when the painting spoke, it found that, away from its master, its voice could not be understood.

From place to place and job to job, the painting went. It hired itself out as a poster so that it could enjoy the warmth of the sun, but it was nailed to a wall and the wind tore at its edges. Cold rains and dark nights covered it, and its brilliant colors began to fade. A man took it down and hung it in his home, where it paled from the sun coming through the windows and absorbed the smoke from the man's cigarettes.

The man tossed the canvas away, and a girl found the painted scene and used it to cover a school book, cracking and creasing its paint. After a year the child pulled off the cover and turned in the book. She tossed the painting into a pile of rags in the school room. The next year, new children came in and used the rags to clean the desks and shelves, coating the painting with dust and grime. The rag was thrown in the trash.

It was picked out by a homeless woman who shuffled by and used it to wipe her nose. Finally even she no longer wanted it, and one cold night, as the woman stood around a burn barrel, she tossed the rag in to keep her warm for a few more minutes.

No sooner did the rag fall and its edges begin to singe than a hand shot into the barrel and yanked it out. It was wrapped in soft cloth. Then all was darkness.

Hours later, the cloth was opened, and the painted scrap found itself in a familiar place. All around it caught glimpses of paintings and sketches. It lay upon a table under the soft light of a lamp, and a gentle hand began to brush and clean it. Burned edges were tenderly cut away and smoke and dirt washed out. Where paint remained, it was reapplied to restore its color. Bare spots and holes were patched from behind and new paint added. Looking up, it could see the artist's eyes, watery with tears but focused with determination. One hand moved deftly across the painting's surface. The other, badly burned, hung useless at the artist's side.

When the restoration was complete, the painting found its voice once more. "Why? Why, Master, did you come and find me?"

"Because I made you for a reason, and that reason did not change, even though you walked away from it. The others you met would use you for the function that seemed best to them, but only I knew the purpose that you were made to fulfill."

"What function, Master?"

"To show the world my heart."

"But now they will never see it. I have ruined everything. You have tried to restore me, Master, but I am not what I once was."

"It is true. You are not what you once were. Now you are something different, but I know that when others see you now—and when you tell them your story—they will truly see my heart."

An Artist with a Purpose

This is our story, or at least a version of it. The Bible tells it in a different way, as the story of a purposeful Creator who gives a purpose to everything created by the divine word and hand. The Bible does not just tell us what, but why.

God created the sky (atmosphere) to separate "water from water" (Genesis 1:6). God created the sun to "govern the day" and the moon to "govern the night," and both lights are to "separate light from darkness" and to "serve as signs to mark sacred times, and days and years" (Genesis 1:14-18). After creating the fish and birds, God commanded them to "fill the water in the seas" and "increase on the earth," so that there would be life in these areas of creation (Genesis 1:22). Then we come to the crown of creation, and God says, "I want someone to bear my image, to represent me, and to rule as my steward." Before we are even created, God starts with our function.

The Bible tells us this is perfectly in keeping with God's character. The Lord is purposeful in every way. When we read through the Scriptures, we find the theme of purpose everywhere. Consider the following verses:

"I make known the end from the beginning,
    from ancient times, what is still to come.
I say, 'My purpose will stand,
    and I will do all that I please.'" (Isaiah 46:10-11)

"God is mighty, but despises no one;
    he is mighty, and firm in his purpose." (Job 36:5)

But the plans of the LORD stand firm forever,
    the purposes of his heart through all generations.
    (Psalm 33:11)

Many are the plans in a person's heart,
    but it is the LORD's purpose that prevails. (Proverbs 19:21)

Because God wanted to make the unchanging nature of
his purpose very clear to the heirs of what was promised,
he confirmed it with an oath. (Hebrews 6:17)

"so is my word that goes out from my mouth:
    It will not return to me empty,

but will accomplish what I desire
and achieve the purpose for which I sent it." (Isaiah 55:11)

He has saved us and called us to a holy life—not because
of anything we have done but because of his own purpose
and grace. This grace was given us in Christ Jesus before
the beginning of time. (2 Timothy 1:9)

The LORD Almighty has sworn,
"Surely, as I have planned, so it will be,
and as I have purposed, so it will happen." (Isaiah 14:24)

The Bible clearly speaks about the purposes of God, but it
also gives frequent examples of God's purpose for individuals. As you might expect, some of these examples are biblical heroes:

Now when David had served God's purpose in his own
generation, he fell asleep. (Acts 13:36)

His [Jesus'] purpose was to create in himself one new hu-
manity out of the two, thus making peace. (Ephesians 2:15)

But God gives a purpose to all, not just to the heroes, and
he plans it ahead of time. Paul describes the case of Jacob and
Esau in Romans 9:11-12: "Yet, before the twins were born or
had done anything good or bad—in order that God's purpose in
election might stand: not by works but by him who calls—she
was told, 'The older will serve the younger.'"

God has a purpose in mind for all, whether they embrace it or
not: "But the Pharisees and the experts in the law rejected God's
purpose for themselves, because they had not been baptized by
John" (Luke 7:30).

Even God's enemies, like Pharaoh, are given a purpose: "But
I have raised you up for this very purpose, that I might show
you my power and that my name might be proclaimed in all the
earth" (Exodus 9:16).

Most Christians know inherently that people were created for a purpose. I often speak to groups about purpose, and when I ask, "What is our purpose?" I usually receive some form of the phrase "to worship God" or "to glorify God." Often someone will quote the Westminster Shorter Catechism, "Man's chief end is to glorify God and to enjoy him forever." This is a great answer, and one we can spend a lifetime working out, but it is not very specific.

People typically come to me with specific questions about what career they should pursue, what major they should study, or what they should spend their lives doing. I can tell them "glorifying God," but I haven't served them very well if I can't give them any more guidance on how to do it.

One practical way to visualize purpose is to stick your nose into your spice cabinet. Examine all of those lovely little jars full of powerful scents and tastes. What is their purpose? Well, the purpose of spices is to make food taste better, right? Based on that definition, I should be able to use any of them interchangeably in any recipe. But if I'm making something Italian, I hope I grab the oregano and not the curry. If instead I am making breakfast rolls, it makes a big difference if I pick cinnamon versus chili powder. Spices have a general purpose and a specific purpose, and so do people.

You were absolutely created to glorify God, but you were created to do so in specific ways, ways that are unique to who you are as an individual. Each of us reflects a bit of God's glory, but God designed each of us to do it differently.

Paul: A Man on a Mission

"This man is my chosen instrument to proclaim my name to the Gentiles and their kings and to the people of Israel." (Acts 9:15)

"Set apart for me Barnabas and Saul for the work to which I have called them." (Acts 13:2)

"For this is what the Lord has commanded us:

'I have made you a light for the Gentiles,
    that you may bring salvation to the ends of the earth.'"
    (Acts 13:47)

Paul is one of the clearest examples we have of someone in Scripture who discovered what he was supposed to be doing with his life. Once God makes clear to Paul his purpose, Paul is open about sharing it. Think about how he introduces himself:

Paul, a servant of Christ Jesus, called to be an apostle
and set apart for the gospel of God . . . we received grace
and apostleship to call people from among the Gentiles.
(Romans 1:1,5)

Paul, called to be an apostle of Christ Jesus by the will of
God. (1 Corinthians 1:1)

And for this purpose I was appointed a herald and an
apostle—I am telling the truth, I am not lying—and a true
and faithful teacher of the Gentiles. (1 Timothy 2:7)

He shows no hesitation, does he? At the time, some other believers must have thought this sounded presumptuous, but Paul was certain of his calling. He knew what function had been given to him. When we've caught a vision for the purpose God has given us, we start to have that same kind of confidence. It is not the arrogance of someone who wants to impress others with his gift. It is the certainty of someone who has received clarity from the Lord and doesn't want anything to distract him from doing what he was built to do.

Paul was specially prepared by God to fulfill his purpose, but the story does not look promising at the beginning. The first time the Bible introduces us to the man who became Paul, apostle to the Gentiles, he was called Saul, persecutor of the early church. In Acts 7, Saul of Tarsus was a witness to the stoning of Stephen, the first martyr among Christ's disciples. From there, Saul launched his own career of searching out the other followers of the Way, arresting them, and handing them over to the Jewish leaders for torture (Acts 8).

When the believers heard about his conversion on the road to Damascus, they were astonished. Any of us living at the time would have voted Paul "Least Likely to Become a Christian." Yet, when we look with spiritual eyes, he was the perfect candidate for God to use. As Paul tells us in Philippians 3:5, he had the best possible pedigree to gain the respect of the Jews of the Roman world, whose synagogues would become the first stops in his journeys. Paul studied with the best teachers and knew the Scriptures forward and backward (Acts 22:3). He had Roman citizenship, which protected him and gave him a hearing on several occasions (Acts 16:35-39; 22:25-29; 23:27). Paul had all the important tools; all he needed was a call from God.

What is this calling that God has pressed on Paul's heart? What is the purpose that drives him? In Romans 15:15-16, Paul tells us:

I have written you quite boldly on some points to remind you of them again, because of the grace God gave me to be a minister of Christ Jesus to the Gentiles. He gave me the priestly duty of proclaiming the gospel of God, so that the Gentiles might become an offering acceptable to God, sanctified by the Holy Spirit.

In verses 20-21 he adds,

It has always been my ambition to preach the gospel where Christ was not known, so that I would not be building on someone else's foundation. Rather, as it is written:

"Those who were not told about him will see,
    and those who have not heard will understand."

Again, to our ears this might sound like pride or competitiveness. Is Paul saying he wants to go to the Gentile lands because he doesn't want to share his success with anyone else? No, this is the voice of someone who has received his orders clearly from the highest authority and knows that he has been given a charge to fulfill. Here is someone who knows his purpose. Paul can see that if he stays to minister to those who have already heard the name of Christ, he is doing work that others can do. Who then will do the work for which he has been specially equipped? His purpose has been kindled inside him, and he knows that to do something else is to hinder God's glory.

John Piper talks about this passage in Romans 15 and describes the profound effect that the verse that Paul quotes (from Isaiah 52:15) has had on him.

> Now here's my take on his understanding of that text in his life. He says, "That verse describes my life. That's why I do what I do." Well, no. He got knocked off his horse on the way to Damascus, that's why he does what he does. But in fact, God, God takes the Bible and with all the other things that happen to us—he burns a specific portion of it into you like he does nobody else. So one of the ways it gets specific, like what field, or what age, or whether you go to school is—you are reading your Bible and something happens to you. It just takes you. You can't leave it. You try to leave it. It won't leave you. It is portions of the Scripture rooting in your soul, and then over time you can't leave it. It will cause some portion of the word to grip you and it will become a decisive moment in your life.[1]

Purpose in Old Pages

God can speak to us about our purpose through our experiences or the words of other people, but he also often speaks to us through his Word. Scripture is "alive and active" (Hebrews 4:12). It is like no other book in the world in its power to speak individually into our lives. As Piper suggests, sometimes when we are reading, a Scripture jumps out at us. The truth of a particular passage resonates with something deep inside us, and we can't let it go.

You may have heard the joke about the man who used the random-flip method of Scripture reading. At a time of crisis, when he needed to know what to do, he flipped open his Bible and pointed to the second part of Matthew 27:5, "Then he went away and hanged himself." Thinking this odd, he quickly flipped again, this time to Luke 10:37, "Go and do likewise." This cured the man of the random-flip method.

While we should not rely on reading tricks, we should be sensitive to hear the Holy Spirit's voice as we read Scripture. You may be reading along when a verse that you never noticed before suddenly becomes piercingly clear, and you instantly feel that through time and space, this verse may have specific application for you.

I have come to believe that one of the best analogies for the Scriptures is that of a mirror. God's Word does not just instruct but also reflects truth to anyone bold enough to look into it. If I look at the Scriptures, if I am honest, the first thing I will see is the dirt on my own face. We all know how mirrors work. I may be oblivious to the fact that my hairline has moved back another inch or that my friend drew a marker-mustache on me when I was asleep on the couch, but when I look in the mirror, suddenly I'm not able to see anything else.

Sometimes I look at the biblical stories of doubt, manipulation, and selfishness and have to say, "Yeah, that's me." At other times, however, I look and see hope. I see people just like me, fumbling toward God, trying to reflect our Creator's image. I see that the desires of my heart are not that different from those who have walked with God in the past. I hear their words and the words of God, and the Spirit inside me says, "Yes! Get up and follow. Nothing has changed God's purpose for God's people."

This mirror can be dangerous, of course, because again, it shows what is in the heart of the reader. When we approach the Scriptures, we are like monks who build the perfect monastery with a great wall to shut out the evil of the world, forgetting that they carry that same evil in with them in their own hearts. The reader who approaches the Bible with the intention of judging it will find judgment everywhere, while the person whose heart is desperate for mercy will find an all-powerful God sleeping humbly in a stable.

The mirror of the Scriptures is incredibly powerful for our purpose here as well. As we approach the Bible, we should keep in our hearts the question that God clearly answered for Paul: What is it that I have been given to do that others cannot do?

This is not an utterance of pride, any more than it was pride that led the apostles to say, "It would not be right for us to neglect the ministry of the word of God in order to wait on tables" (Acts 6:2). It is a question of purpose. Why would we do what we can clearly see others are already doing around us, but neglect the duty we have been given? We will not accomplish someone else's purpose as well as our own, and someone else will have to perform ours.

What Scripture verses have arrested your attention? You might not have one verse that speaks specifically to a function, but there are probably patterns in the verses and stories you love most. It is worth taking a moment, putting this book down, and writing down a list of your favorite verses. What connection do you see? What aspect of God or what need of God's people runs like a thread through many of your favorite passages? That may indicate what part of God's glory you are built to reveal. We read those verses, and it is like the Holy Spirit has sounded us like a gong and our souls reverberate in answer.

Passing on Your Gift

I remember when I first started thinking about the idea of finding God's purpose for my life many years ago. In my research, I stumbled across Colossians 2:2-3, which says, "My goal [purpose] is that they may be encouraged in heart and united in love, so that they may have the full riches of complete understanding, in order that they may know the mystery of God, namely, Christ, in whom are hidden all the treasures of wisdom and knowledge." Obviously, the word *purpose* leaped from the page, but it was what came after it that captured me. I felt like the passage was speaking directly to me.

Each phrase seemed to connect with an aspect of my own personality or character. For example, I'm one of those strange people who love to take inventories of all kinds. I've completed several spiritual-gift assessments, and I always score highest in encouragement ("encouraged in heart"). My friends give me a hard time because I always have an analogy or some type of visual picture to share with people to help them understand complex ideas ("so that they may have the full riches of complete understanding"). In fact, I would say one of my favorite activities in the world is to help others draw out who they are, and who God has created them to be ("in order that they may know the mystery of God"). I'm a purpose-finder. This whole book, and indeed much of my work, is about encouraging others to get a deeper understanding of the mysterious work that God has done and is doing in their lives.

I sat and read this verse four or five times, and it gave me chills. Since that time, I have carried Colossians 2:2-3 with me into many projects. Reading it always reminds me of what I feel God wants me to spend my time doing.

Just this past week I had lunch with three younger men from my office. They are at an age when they are all looking ahead and thinking of what it will be like to start families. As the only one in the group with kids, I was the natural target for their questions. What started as a few inquiries about schooling options turned into quite a conversation about how to invest in your family and about the inevitable personality conflicts that come up. It was not long before I was instinctually using personality theory to help them think about how to minimize friction in their family relationships. Pretty soon, I went around the group and described each one by saying, "This is how I see you. Is that correct? I think this is where you get your energy. This is what you like about the guy sitting next to you, but this is when he drives you crazy, right?"

They are all nodding their heads and saying, "Wow, that is totally true. Dude, you do drive me crazy when you do that." One of them said, "Cool, we've just been sitting at the feet of Aaron learning."

I immediately bristled. The little alarm bell went off in my head and a warning said, "Pride, pride! You must act modest."

I started to fumble through some kind of humble-sounding brush-off, and then caught myself. That would be totally dishonest. I started over.

"What I should say is that God made me that way. I am thrilled if you received something good from our talk. Whatever I have that helped is something God gave to me, and now I've had the opportunity to give it to you, and God's gift gets passed on. So don't look at me. It's all God's fault!"

NOTES

1. John Piper, "Finish the Mission for the Joy of All People," Desiring God conference, September 24, 2011. See http://www.desiringgod.org/conference-messages/speaker-panel-david-platt-michael-ramsden-michael-oh-ed-stetzer-john-piper (accessed May 15, 2014).

CHAPTER 5

Armed and Dangerous

The Purpose Finder Assessment

Dad was a philosopher and had what he called his Theory of Purpose, which held that everything in life had a purpose, and unless it achieved that purpose, it was just taking up space on the planet and wasting everybody's time. —JEANNETTE WALLS, *HALF BROKE HORSES*[1]

For it is God who works in you to will and to act in order to fulfill his good purpose. —PHILIPPIANS 2:13

I can hear her from well down the marbled hall.

"Good morning, honey, how are you? Let me give you a hug, sweetie. You look nice today. I like that shirt. Look at you, aren't you handsome? Do you have a presentation today?"

That is Miss Barbara, the cashier at the university cafeteria. She is a legend on campus, and she is irrefutable proof that your title has no bearing on the effect you can have when you are using your Purpose. Miss Barbara greets every student who comes through the dining hall line with love and enthusiasm. She hugs them, she makes a fuss over them, she asks them how they are, and with her tone, her words, and her actions she tells them that she considers each one of them special.

Two years ago, one of my favorite students graduated. He was selected to give the graduation speech to the faculty, his peers, and the many families in attendance. In his speech, he included many of the things you would expect—remembering the past, celebrating the present, imagining the future—but one piece stood out to me. He also dedicated a paragraph or two to Miss Barbara. He pointed to her as one of the highlights of his college career, and as a symbol of what was best about the university. I have heard so many students say the same thing. Maybe they are only one of a thousand students she sees each day, but her joy and enthusiasm make them feel like she has been waiting all day just for them.

Recently, Miss Barbara was recognized by the leaders of the university with a special staff award. In front of a big crowd of administrators, she looked shy and somehow surprised that she was being honored for being herself. I could tell that the award was nice, but not half as important to her as the daily hugs from the students she greets. Somewhere along the way, she had decided that her Purpose is to care for each student the way she would want her own children to be cared for when they were away from home. Living from that Purpose has affected the lives of hundreds of students, and you can tell by seeing her in action that living from your Purpose is often its own reward.

> *Adhere to your purpose and you will soon feel as well as you ever did. On the contrary, if you falter, and give up, you will lose the power of keeping any resolution, and will regret it all your life.* —Abraham Lincoln[2]

We each have a Purpose, but we will never truly understand it until we seek to understand it from God. In this chapter, I will take you through an exercise that will help you discover your Purpose through a series of questions, based on the concept of looking for God's fingerprints in your life. The ultimate goal of this exercise is to develop a purpose statement. Just as most companies have a purpose statement or mission statement to guide their decision making, so we as individuals need a statement of purpose to remind us what actions we should be taking to fulfill our function. As I began developing this set of questions years ago, I created my first purpose statement, which I still use today.

I consider my Purpose "to help others see who they are and imagine who they can become." It is a simple but effective way of reminding me how I should spend my time and energy. The "to" statement reminds me that a Purpose is about action. I like to use the theme of a light bulb and illumination in much of my work. For me the idea of a light bulb igniting is a visual picture of this purpose statement. When I am using my Purpose, I help light bulbs go on for others.

Purpose is about who you are, but it is expressed in what you do. Whenever I feel drained or frustrated in projects I'm working on, I step back and ask myself, "Am I spending time helping others see and imagine, or am I bogged down in other tasks that have nothing to do with my special equipping?" While I can't spend all my time doing this one activity, I had better spend at least some of my time doing it, or I am in the wrong place.

It's Not Your Job, It's Your Purpose

Sometimes our Purpose leads up to one great event that the world recognizes, like Abraham Lincoln's commitment to holding together the Union, or Susan B. Anthony's struggle for women's right to vote, or Rosa Parks's refusal to give up her bus seat. In most cases, however, it is less about one big accomplishment than it is about living out who you were born to be and doing what you were built to do every day and everywhere you find yourself. Don't think of your Purpose as your job title, although I would argue your job should help you achieve your Purpose whenever possible. Purpose is often what makes you good at certain jobs.

Think of tools in a toolbox. What is the purpose of a hammer? To pound nails (or pull them back out). It is perfectly suited to its job. Can you use it for other things? You can try. Use it to drive screws, chop down trees, or paint walls with if you like, but you will find it is not very effective. You will be a frustrated hammer user, and if your hammer could talk, it would tell you it is not too happy with you either. A hammer should spend its time pounding nails. The same goes for screwdrivers, saws, and tape measures.

They all have a purpose for which they are uniquely suited, and they function best when they do it.

If you are a hammer, you should be pounding nails. If you know that, you can look around for the opportunities God has given you to do so. Living from your Purpose will bring God joy and glory and you satisfaction. That's not to say there are no choices. A hammer can be used to build a house, construct a park bench, or hang up pictures, just as in life you may use your gifts and Purpose in different jobs and roles. But to know what work you should be doing, you must understand your Purpose (pounding nails).

If you've followed me so far, the questions you should be asking are, "Okay, so what tool am I?" and "What does pounding nails (or painting walls, or driving screws) look like for me?"

The Purpose Finder is a subjective assessment, with no right or wrong answers. It is not intended to give you an exact match with a specific job title but to help you to pinpoint the special role God has given you within God's kingdom and the greater world.

Tips for Using the Assessment

- Answer each question thoughtfully, with as much detail as possible, preferably written down. After each answer, ask whether you have answered the "Why?" question. Why did I choose this response? Why do I prefer this choice?

- Ask two other people you trust to answer these same questions about you. Ideally, one would be a parent or family member who has known you well since you were very young. Often God's design on our hearts is evident very early, before it has been obscured by other life experiences. The other person could be a friend who knows you well now. Compare their answers with your answers to find themes or to think of some things you do naturally and don't consider that special. Often others will see them as very special indeed.

- Follow the instructions after the assessment for help in identifying themes and creating a purpose statement.

- Over the next few weeks, pray about the possible purpose statement(s) you have created. Get feedback from others about whether what you have come up with accurately reflects who you are and what you do.

- Apply it to your choices. Learn all you can about what careers and roles will best allow you to use this Purpose (more about this below).

The Purpose Finder Assessment

1. What positive personality traits did your parents pass on to you—traits that you *like* in yourself?

2. What minor things did you get in trouble for when you were younger?

3. What role did you play in your family growing up? (For example: Were you the caretaker of siblings? Were you the peacemaker? Were you the one who planned family adventures?) What role do you play now?

4. List three high points in your life and the reason why they were so memorable. These should be moments when you really felt you were "on" or were using your gifts, but they don't have to be huge accomplishments.
   *
   *
   *

5. List one or two "best moments" you have experienced in the last week and the reasons why.

    *

    *

6. Name a past job or high-school or college class that you did not enjoy. Be as specific as possible about why it was not a good match. Give examples. (For example: It bothered me to deal with people's problems all day. The class was too theoretical. I hated being cooped up in an office all day.)

7. In your daily activities, do you most enjoy working with people (teaching, serving, providing care), ideas (writing, doing research, experimenting), or objects (operating machines, building, cooking)? Rank these three in your order of preference.

    1.

    2.

    3.

8. Why do your friends seek you out for help? Do they come to you for acceptance? Is it because they can count on you? If they were asked what your best qualities are, what would they say?

9. What one thing that you do would gain even your enemy's respect? (For example, if someone did not like you, that person might say, "Well, he or she drives me crazy, but at least . . . he

is honest, she fights for what she believes in, he's a great cook, she's an amazing carpenter.")

10. What do people thank you for? (For example, the quality of your work, your kindness, your ability to lighten the mood, your helpful advice, your generosity with time or resources.)

11. If you could be internationally recognized for doing one good thing, what would it be?

Finding Your Themes

Once you have written out the answers to your assessment and given it out to a couple of people who know you well, it is time to look for clues. What are the threads that run through your answers that will help you get a clearer sense of your Purpose? As you review your answers, I encourage you to have paper or a notebook handy to record any themes you find and to answer the follow-up questions in this section.

As strange as it may sound, start with question 7. People usually have a clear initial reaction to this question about favorite activities and find it easy to answer. The key here is that your two first choices will typically work in some combination in your Purpose, with your first choice leading. Just as important, you can probably clear a large number of jobs and roles off the table by eliminating things related to your third selection.

For example, my first two choices are people and ideas. Objects are a clear third choice. That means I can pretty confidently eliminate jobs or roles that involve hands-on manipulation of objects (construction, repair, many areas of hands-on science, much manufacturing and assembly, areas of engineering, managing supplies). It is a good confirmation that when I hear these types of jobs, they don't stir any interest.

If your third choice is people, you can probably eliminate areas of customer service, counseling, teaching, nursing, sales, hospitality industries, or human services. If your third area is ideas, steer clear of research, writing, higher education, and most areas of traditional science (biology, chemistry, or physics). Think for a minute about what areas you can safely eliminate.

Now let's look at questions 1 through 3, which explore your childhood and family dynamics. Sometimes God's fingerprints show clearly very early in life. Some people whose Purpose may be to care for others in some area of health or wellness began by bandaging stuffed animals at an early age. Others were constantly inventing unconventional solutions, memorizing everything they saw, or creating harmony between people in conflict. Getting some feedback about what traits you have always had can be helpful. Looking for family traits can also be useful. If there are some things you like about yourself that were clearly passed on to you from your parents or grandparents, they may be clues.

Perhaps my favorite question of all is number 3, which essentially asks, "What did you get in trouble for doing?" I described in chapter 3 the insights I gleaned about myself by reflecting on this question. I could share many other examples. For instance, I had a classmate in high school who was the most creative class clown you can imagine. Now he's working in Hollywood at a movie studio.

Now think about some of those important moments that have helped to teach you who you are. Your answers to questions 4 and 5 are essential. What you are looking for is a theme or themes among the moments you identify as best. Why did you feel so "on" at these moments? What were you doing? If you had to describe what kind of tool you were in those moments, what would you say? If your answer varies depending on the moment, is there a connection between those types of tools? Are you using any of those same types of skills on a daily basis and enjoying them? Where do you get your energy day to day?

Conversely, check your answer for question 6. What does it say about what drains your energy? Does this seem like the opposite of what you found in questions 4 and 5? Does it fit into the area you chose last in question 7? What themes do you notice about what energizes and inspires you?

Think about your life now. Read your answers to questions 8 through 10. How do others perceive you? What do you do really well? If your friends or enemies had to pick a Purpose for you, or a set of best skills, what would they say? Sometimes your gifts—making others feel comfortable, speaking persuasively, inspiring confidence, breaking problems into logical steps, providing a listening ear—seem so natural to you that they don't stand out. Knowing how you affect others when you do what you do best can reveal a lot about what your special equipping may be.

Finally, think about the future with question 11. If you had no concerns about making money, or earning a prestigious job title, or impressing others with your professional identity and achievements, what skills would you want to use on a daily basis? Which of your skills and talents could you use every day and feel energized rather than drained? What would you most want to be remembered for doing? At the end of your life, you would want to describe yourself as someone who always . . . (looked out for those in need; helped others understand each other better; discovered truths that improved our knowledge of the world).

Purpose Statement

Taking the information you have written above, begin forming your answers into patterns. Where do you see things that match? Maybe you see several questions that indicate you like to discover things—solutions, the answers to puzzles, what happens when you combine chemicals. Maybe you find you are always taking care of people and helping them feel better. Or maybe you are the person others come to for expertise when they need something put together correctly. Do you enjoy doing these things? How can you put them into an action sentence?

Starting with the word *to*, begin making the theme you picked out into a phrase that best describes what you do well and love doing. Here are some examples:

To use care and compassion to help hurting people
    feel better

To build things with excellence that people will
    marvel at

To uncover secrets in the world around us

To bring order into all the environments where I live
    and work

To listen and give good advice that will improve
    people's lives

To help people see unfairness and injustice and inspire
    them to change it

To create a business organization that honors God and
    helps others support their families

To help people use technology to make their lives better

To help children see and reach their potential

To make connections across culture that lead to better
    relationships

To bring harmony into conflict situations

You probably will not draft a statement that resonates with you right away. Keep writing. Don't be afraid to throw a bunch of possibilities on paper. Sometimes it takes a page full of ideas before the right one pops out.

List your best possible purpose statements—in a journal, on a piece of notebook paper, on the inside cover or margin of this book. When you have something you like, test it. Ask yourself:

1. Could I really use this skill or do this thing in the major areas of my life and enjoy it?

2. Is this something that, if I do it right, will bring glory to God too?

3. Can this Purpose be transferred to multiple jobs or roles? (For example, "to be a doctor" is not a Purpose, but "to help people recover from pain" or "to help others live healthier lives" might be.)

4. When I use this skill do I feel energized or exhausted?

If your purpose statement passes this test, take it to God. Ask the Holy Spirit to tell you if you are on the right track. Your words may not be exactly correct, but often God will confirm or gently correct you through the Word, through others, or through the Spirit's work in your heart. If you have others whom you trust, ask them to pray for you about it as well.

What did you hear? Record any insights or epiphanies in a journal or on a note in your smartphone—somewhere you can refer to it and remind yourself of God's word to you about your Purpose.

Now comes the exciting challenge of applying your Purpose. As you go about your daily tasks, remind yourself of your purpose statement. Ask yourself if the activity you are doing is utilizing that Purpose. How could you incorporate more opportunities to do what you do best into your day? How does knowing your purpose statement help you see your work differently?

Let's say you are an administrative assistant. Before knowing your Purpose, you might say that your job is to screen phone calls, take notes, organize files, keep a calendar, and prepare reports. After exploring your Purpose, you might realize that you've been gifted with helping other people perform their jobs more efficiently and effectively. Understanding your Purpose in this way might help you see how all of these separate tasks fit together into a bigger picture—one in which you become a champion for the people around you. Knowing who you are increases both your satisfaction and your effect.

This is the "who" and "what" of your Function. Who are you and what should you be doing? You should be living and working from your Purpose. Purpose is the most important building block in your Function, but it is only the first step.

NOTES

1. Jeannette Walls. *Half Broke Horses* (New York: Scribner, 2009), 24.
2. *The Collected Works of Abraham Lincoln* edited by Roy P. Basler, Volume V, "Letter to Quintin Campbell" (June 28, 1862), 288.

CHAPTER 6

Get Inspired

Answering the "Where?" Question

Nothing is really work unless you would rather be doing something else. —JAMES BARRIE, DRAMATIST, CREATOR OF *PETER PAN*[1]

"But my servant Caleb—this is a different story. He has a different spirit; he follows me passionately. I'll bring him into the land that he scouted and his children will inherit it." —(NUMBERS 14:24, THE MESSAGE)

A few years ago, I was teaching a class on career management and thought the group would benefit from the perspective of a recent graduate. I invited a student I had known several years before to speak to us via video conference. This smart, vivacious young woman is a PhD candidate in epidemiology and public health at Harvard.

She told her story and advised the class about the importance of being willing to reassess and adjust your path to make sure you are in the right place. Once they found that right place, she counseled, be bold and network with passion. She advised the group to take the time now to explore and understand who they are, saying, "It is interesting. I have thought a lot about how to make good decisions, balancing what looks like a fit with your feelings. It is tough, because you may be looking on the one hand at something that makes sense and on the other at something that keeps calling to you."

Inspiration is the second piece of your Function. There is a place where what you are best at doing (Purpose) and what you never get tired of doing (Inspiration) intersect. Job experience, even part-time work or summer jobs, can teach you much about the importance of Inspiration.

Working for the Muppets

My first serious summer job did not get off to a good start. My dad connected me with a couple of private contract painters who worked on houses near the beach, about a thirty-minute drive from my house. I had not been driving very long, but I had my own inexpensive car and was proud of my independence. I was usually a pretty responsible kid, but that day I certainly didn't show it. Maybe I was just nervous, but I underestimated the amount of time it would take me to get to the meeting spot and showed up late. Even worse, I had run out of time to put gas in my car and showed up with an empty tank. The first day on the job, my new bosses had to give me money to fill up my tank to get to the job site. Not exactly employee of the month material!

I spent the summer making it up to them, though. I worked tirelessly in the sun in the muggy July and August heat. I learned to follow directions, and I practiced doing things to meet their standards. There was a right way to clean a brush, one way to sand correctly, and one correct technique for painting a window.

The job was a great match for me for the summer. It gave me a lot of time to think without disruption, which is something I still value today. I learned to work hard and take pride in it. I also realized, however, that for my career I would want something with more people interaction and room for personal growth. I was not going to be able to use my natural love of helping people grow assisting two guys, whom I really liked working for but who reminded me of Statler and Waldorf, the hecklers in *The Muppet Show*.

This kind of "doing" is incredibly helpful for testing what inspires you and what does not. Any summer job, part-time work, or volunteer experience can be incredibly useful if you use it as an opportunity to evaluate whether you have a passion for any part of what you are doing. You may not love everything about the work, but are there aspects that resonate with you?

I once heard the well-known theorist John Krumboltz speak to a group of career counselors about the importance of action in the career process. The gist of his talk was to encourage students to get out and make something happen—anything happen. Krumboltz's Happenstance Learning Theory teaches that it is in action that we learn how to make career decisions in a complex and rapidly changing environment. If we are alert as we try new experiences and use different skills, we are open and flexible when unexpected opportunities present themselves.[2]

In his talk, Krumboltz suggested that the worst thing to do is to stay still, paralyzed by indecision. As so many mothers have cajoled at the dinner table, "Try it, you might like it!" We often live with a terrible fear that we are going to get our career decision wrong. The refreshingly good news on this front is that career planning is not just one decision. I think that is one of the misconceptions that Krumboltz best disputes.

Career discovery is a process of making choices and being open to learning from them. It is a path of looking for God's fingerprints and following God's voice. We are often more motivated by fear of getting it wrong than an interest in getting it right, and this leads to all kinds of missed opportunities.

You have probably heard that the average college student changes majors about three times. The dynamic doesn't stop there. Many people don't make a good first choice of a job. Some know what they would like to do but can't find an opening. Others think they know what they want but later realize it is a bad match. Some job searchers hate searching so much they take the first job they can get. Is all hope lost? Of course not. They can still use the job they do find to discover what inspires them so that they can move closer to getting paid to do it.

Learning by doing is also a great tool for differentiating between an Inspiration and an interest, which can be difficult. We all have interests and hobbies. I like Kung Fu movies, Greek food, playing the guitar, and reading, but I would not consider any of these the source of my Inspiration. They are hobbies or preferences that I might spend time on in a given week, but they are not the kinds of things that will inspire me to greatness over a lifetime.

Interests are short-lived. You may have a friend who enjoys making crafts or playing sports, and for a season, you might also devote energy to that activity. When the relationship changes or some other activity comes along that seems more appealing, however, the old interest is filed away as "a good experience." You may take up something for a few months until it becomes difficult, expensive, or inconvenient, at which point it quietly dies off. That is an interest.

Hobbies may stick with you for a lifetime, but they fail to inspire you to greatness. Watching movies is one of my favorite hobbies and has been for as long as I can remember, but my joy in them is just in receiving. I don't have a burning, life-altering desire to make movies that will change the world. If I suddenly lost my sight and could not watch movies anymore, I would miss them. I would not, however, feel as if some great part of my being was left unfulfilled. Hobbies are something that you do for you. An Inspiration is something that you do for the rest of the world or because you feel it must be done.

This is one of the great traps of career planning. Many people cannot recognize the difference between an interest or hobby and an Inspiration. They love riding horses or singing or playing computer games, so they plan a career based on that activity. Later they realize that it was a passing phase or that they enjoyed that activity for relaxation. Now that they continually have to do it, they no longer enjoy it.

The Impulse of Inspiration

I like to think of an Inspiration as the impulse that motivates a great mission. We can all think of historical figures who stood for some great idea and changed the world because of a passion for it. William Wilberforce fought passionately for the abolition of slavery. It was a difficult fight that cost him money, friends, and years of his life. If it had been based on an interest, it would have dissipated when he faced what seemed like impossible odds. If it had been a hobby, it would never have propelled him to dramatic action. Wilberforce's success was based on the combination of his passion for justice for the slaves and his gifts, which God used at the right moment in time to make an enormous impact.

The same could be said of any number of other great figures. Martin Luther King Jr.'s passion for freedom and equality or Mother Teresa's quest to show the love of Jesus to the poorest of the poor are other examples of people whose passions moved the world. But these monumental missions did not start as fully grown ideas. They began as simple Inspirations. They began when someone said, "This isn't right. Somebody should do something about this." And that person began in a small way to do something about it.

An Inspiration does not have to be something that lofty. In a 2007 interview with Bill Gates (Microsoft) and Steve Jobs (Apple) at the D5 technology conference, Gates was asked about what he saw as his legacy. He answered by stating what I characterize as his Inspiration:

> Well, the most important work I got a chance to be involved in, no matter what I do, is the personal computer. You know, that's what I grew up, in my teens, my 20s, my 30s, you know, I even knew not to get married until later because I was so obsessed with it. That's my life's work. And it's lucky for me that some of the skills and resources—but I put skills first—that I was able to develop through those experiences can be applied to the benefit of the people who haven't had technology, including medicine, working for them. So it's an incredible blessing to have two things like that. But the thing that I'll, you know, if you look inside my brain, it's filled with software and, you know, the magic of software and the belief in software and, you know, that's not going to change.[3]

Instead of waning over time, like an interest would, Gates's Inspiration grew. What started as a garage project began to grow into a pattern of sustained, passionate pursuit, until it became a mission.

Gates's personal Inspiration to make software accessible to everyone became his company's inspiration, too. In 1975, Microsoft wrote down a goal statement of "a computer on every desk and in every home."[4] Gates went on to become the richest man alive and an incredible philanthropist, but he was clear in his interview that those were never his goals. It was about being inspired by what you do.

In the same interview, Steve Jobs agreed.

> People say you have to have a lot of passion for what you're doing and it's totally true. And the reason is because it's so hard that if you don't, any rational person would give up. It's really hard. And you have to do it over a sustained period of time. So if you don't love it, if you're not having fun doing it, you don't really love it, you're going to give up. And that's what happens to most people, actually. If you really look at the ones that ended up, you know, being "successful" in the eyes of society and the ones that didn't, oftentimes, it's the ones [who] were successful loved what they did so they could persevere, you know, when it got really tough. And the ones that didn't love it quit because they're sane, right? Who would want to put up with this stuff if you don't love it?[5]

The key is that the idea that sparked passion in these two men had staying power. The idea stuck with them, haunted them, tantalized them, and inspired them to take action. Something about the idea resonated with them so deeply that they were willing to step out and take a risk—sometimes a very big one—to make the idea become a reality.

These two titans found their Inspiration not in a great moral cause but in a practical field—technology. Yet both of them have had an incredible impact on the lives of millions around the world. Their Inspirations have changed all of our lives.

Warning! This Could Happen to You

You may have just that kind of a small idea. You aren't thinking of how you can change the world, but you can see how things would be better if something were different. That idea keeps coming back to you, nagging you, inspiring you to take action. You may start by thinking about how it would affect you. Why can't medicine taste good? What if there were less traffic? What if I could send the vegetables I don't like to hungry people in another country? But the question sticks with you, and you start to envision how the world would be different if you were able to make a change. Then you start to live differently because of that idea.

Let me give you an example of one of my greatest Inspirations. When I began my first real job, in college admissions, my learning grew exponentially, and I was able to refine my understanding of who I was and what skills I should be using. I loved communicating with others in a way that conveyed meaning and helped them understand. I found myself drawn to speaking and writing, not the mechanics of communication, but as tools to help people toward a better understanding of themselves. Even in general conversations, I often used movies or analogies to help others see an idea more clearly and to recognize how the notion applied to them. Most of all, I loved helping people discover who they could become.

One of my favorite projects was the building of a tour guide program. Almost every college has a group of student ambassadors who walk people around campus when they come to visit. This group is important, as prospective students often make their choice about where they will attend based on this experience. The school I was working for at the time had had a lot of problems with its tour group and needed an overhaul, and I was tapped to make it happen.

I dismantled the previous program. Then I selected a core group of about thirty students and set about creating what I imagined would be a customer service masterpiece. When I began, my sights were on getting results, but along the way I discovered professional development and mentoring. More valuable to me than the quality improvements or the many successes we achieved was the opportunity to invest in and have an influence on those thirty students. I was determined that these bright, young ambassadors would get every opportunity to build their professional skills and run the program as their own. In particular, I created a leadership group of seven students whom I mentored in every way I knew how. It was a powerful recipe. This program had tremendous success, but more importantly, it had an impact on their lives and on mine.

I still communicate with some of those students. It is so much fun to see all the amazing things they are doing and to remember the time we worked together. A few of them have sent me terrific emails telling me how much I influenced their professional development. I consider those messages some of the greatest honors I have ever received.

This theme of mentoring and professional development has followed me ever since. Once I put a name to it, I began to recognize that most of my favorite parts of all the jobs I have had are a form of it. When I advise others in their careers, I am mentoring. When I write or speak, I am providing professional development to a larger audience. It is all a part of connecting with people to help them understand and grow.

The best part is that I never get tired of working in my Inspiration. Not long ago, I was looking at my schedule, lamenting a little that I didn't seem to have thirty minutes free anywhere. Then I received an email from a student I had mentored in a previous semester, asking for advice. Somehow the thirty minutes appeared in my schedule.

I make time for those I consider mentees. I can talk for hours about how people with different temperaments view the world (and sometimes bore my family to tears). Any magazine, no matter how dull the normal subject matter, can suck me in by advertising a personality test on the cover. I love to see people grow! If you visit my website (www.aaronbasko.com), you'll see that most of my blogs are about mentoring or professional development in one form or another, whether lessons I have learned or ideas I think will help someone else. When I develop a resource the goal is to mentor others—people I could never reach face to face.

Connecting the Dots

What is it that never gets old for you? That you never take for granted? That is another important clue to the Purpose you've been given. Practice answering these questions. Go to a bookstore and browse. What section do you find yourself drawn to irresistibly? What magazine do you want to read cover to cover? If you could pick only one blog or website to visit of all your favorites, which would it be? Once you know what area you are passionate about, why would you want to work in something else?

Finding your Inspiration takes a little bit of effort, but the clues are all around you. While Purpose is that skill you want to use over and over again, Inspiration is that idea that captures your attention and keeps coming back. There is a consistency to it, and it grows and matures as you do.

I will often ask people I am advising to write down a list of the significant experiences or actions from their lives. What activities do they love and why? What were the turning points when they chose one interest over another and why? Were there books or movies that changed their thinking? Did they ever receive special recognition for something that they accomplished? What are the proudest moments they can remember? What did they learn from each major experience?

Next, I ask them to look at the list and connect the dots. Typically their answers create very strong themes. One person's significant experiences might revolve around problem solving, teamwork, and travel. Another person might list activities related to caring for others and expressing creativity. A few of the themes are inevitably hobbies, not something they could do for work or would even want to, but other areas will match elegantly into areas of Inspiration.

Try this for yourself. Make a list of your most important memories, experiences, and activities. Now imagine that you have to sort each item on your list into one of four boxes. How would you group them? What label would you put on each box (music, family, achievement, competition, service, education, communicating, spiritual growth, entrepreneurship)?

When I complete this exercise myself, the theme of professional development jumps to the forefront. The professional accomplishments I'm most proud of and the activities I enjoy—teaching career classes, speaking to groups, writing about topics that help people grow, conducting training, mentoring people—connect to each other around the idea of helping others develop and gain insight and wisdom. I have other groupings around family and music, both of which are important to me, but they are not likely to be a career.

Another area of Inspiration that stands out on my list is connecting with others across cultures. This is an idea that has repeated itself frequently in my life in many different forms, from that first conversation with my new Cuban friend on the airplane, to my year as an exchange student, to my love of learning foreign languages and my enjoyment of international recruitment travel. There is something about connecting with people from other cultures and increasing understanding that always draws me back.

What should I do with the contents of my boxes? Clearly I have two main themes, and one seems a bit stronger than the other. Both have been consistent in my life and have grown over time. Can they help me find a career?

If these are the passions I will never get tired of, let's examine whether I could make a living at them. We'll cover this in more detail in the next chapter, but for now, can you think of people who make a living helping other people with their professional development? I can. Teachers, trainers, coaches, and counselors all help others with their professional development. What about increasing cross-cultural understanding? Yes, diplomats, international student advisors, cross-cultural trainers, translators, consultants, and missionaries all help people from different cultures make connections. So clearly both of my Inspirations could lead to a professional career, and perhaps there is even some way I could combine them.

Rank your boxes by how many events or experiences they contain. If any boxes contain only one or two items, you may have found a hobby. If one or two of your boxes are full of experiences that follow a consistent theme in your life, you may have discovered an Inspiration. When you think you have a few possible candidates, test them out with any of the following exercises.

The Three-Movies Exercise

One of my favorite warm-up exercises to help people begin thinking about Inspiration is called the Three-Movies Exercise. It has been used by many different people, but I first came across it as a post by author Mary DeMuth on the blog of Michael Hyatt, former chair of Tommy Nelson Publishing.[6] To identify what inspires you, list your three favorite movies. Now think for a moment about what common theme runs through all three. What is the shared story line? This story line quite often mimics where your Inspiration lies.

When I first did this exercise, I couldn't choose just three movies, but the four I listed were *The Matrix*, *The Lord of the Rings*, *The Thirteenth Warrior*, and *The Last Samurai*. Of course the first common element I thought of was that they are all action movies, and most of them involve a lot of swords. Since I was pretty sure I wasn't going to be a sword maker, I knew I had to dig deeper.

As I thought about the story line, I realized that all four movies contained a common plot element that resonated with me. Each story started with an unlikely hero. Each of these heroes doubted his ability to rise to the challenge that confronted him. In each story, however, the underdeveloped hero encounters a wise mentor who invests in him. Each mentor sees the hero's potential and helps to forge him into the champion he was meant to be. *Mentoring champions*. As soon as I said those words to myself, I knew this exercise worked! That is, indeed, what inspires me: developing others so that they can become who they were created to be.

What are your favorite movies, or if you are not a frequent movie watcher, what are your favorite books? Who are the heroes of these stories? What is the challenge they face as the story begins? How do they rise to the challenge or grow during the plot in a way that allows them to overcome?

That is why we love art like this, and great stories in particular. When the ending gives you chills, the middle is giving you clues. Take a moment to write down and analyze your picks, and if you can't see the immediate pattern, share them with a few friends.

Ask them if they can see what connects your favorite stories, and if they think that fits you. Frankly, apart from being a great Inspiration-finding warm-up, it is fun. Feel free to use it at the next office party!

Inspiration Questions

When I'm trying to help someone identify his or her Inspiration, I often ask a set of questions to pull out the possibilities. I used a few of these questions at the beginning of the chapter, but here is how I typically ask them:

1. If you had ten minutes to spend in a bookstore but could spend it in only one section, where would you go? What books would you pick?

2. What magazines would you read cover to cover?

3. If you had to have a four-hour class once a week but could pick any topic, what would you choose?

4. Do your friends ever get tired of hearing you talk about a specific topic? If you were to stay up late talking about a subject, what would keep you up?

5. If you could learn anything from any person, who would you choose?

6. What was the last documentary you watched or the last two nonfiction books you read?

Jot down your answers and then look for themes. Most people find that their answers to these questions are very similar and lend good evidence to what they really love.

Rank Your Interests

Another good way to cut through the fog and separate your Inspiration from a long list of interests and hobbies is to force yourself to rank what you love. Start by making an exhaustive list of all of your interests. What do you enjoy doing? How would you like to spend more time? What are your favorite subject areas? Now begin by comparing the first item on your list with the second.

Imagine that you can keep one only item. Whichever interest you don't select will no longer be a part of your life. You won't be able to participate in it again in the future.

When you've chosen the one that you will keep, move down to the next interest on your list until only two choices remain. Now, be honest with yourself. Are these items something you can earn a living at or things you do for fun? To be amazing at them, would you give up all of the other interests on your list if you had to do so?

When you searched for your Purpose, you were seeking to answer the "what" question, "What was I built to do?" It showed you the special skill you could use consistently to make maximum impact. With your Inspiration, you are identifying an answer to the "where" question, "Where do I want to use this skill?"

The field you never tire of learning about and the idea that inspires you to action are what will help you find satisfaction in what you do, even when things get challenging. Your Inspiration provides the context for you to use your Purpose and make a difference.

My Inspiration tells me that I need to work in an organizational setting where I will be surrounded by people who need that kind of mentoring. I need to find an environment full of undiscovered heroes who I can help become champions. If I want to enjoy it, I should look for a field where there is an opportunity to work with people across cultural boundaries and to use my Purpose to make international connections.

Where do your results tell you to work? The answers to your questions might have been about who is important to you. You may have a passion for working with kids, or older adults, or the musically gifted, or scientists, or broken families, or organizations that sell a product you love. Or, your answers may have been more environmental. You should work outside, or in the sports field, or in a large corporation with an active social network, or in a quiet space like a library, or in a small organization with a family feel. Your answer might also have been about mission. The idea that calls to you might be about making a specific difference, such as sharing your faith, or meeting the physical needs or other people, or improving the environment, or building better software, or sharing your enjoyment of animals. All of these answers tell you where you should be looking to apply your special gifts.

When you've clarified these first two pieces of PIE—Purpose (I should use this gift) and Inspiration (in this environment)—you are ready to move on to the third piece: Earnings. In the next chapter you will learn more about how to make a living doing what you love and were built to do.

NOTES

1. Shane Snow, "Finding Your Passion at Work: Twenty Awesome Quotes," LinkedIn, July 4, 2013.

2. John D. Krumboltz, "The Happenstance Learning Theory," *Journal of Career Assessment* (2009): 17, 135, http://www.stanford.edu/~jdk/Happenstance LearningTheory2009.pdf.

3. "D5 Transcript: Gates, Jobs Reminisce," *The Wall Street Journal*, May 31, 2007, http://online.wsj.com/article/SB118063909956120356.html.

4. "Gates, Jobs Reminisce."

5. "Gates, Jobs Reminisce."

6. Mary DeMuth, guest post on www.michaelhyatt.com, May 3, 2011, http://michaelhyatt.com/find-your-passion-in-three-steps.html.

CHAPTER 7

Your Earnings Equation

Answering the "How?" Question

There is no future in any job. The future lies in the person who holds the job. —GEORGE W. CRANE[1]

From the fruit of their lips people are filled with good things, and the work of their hands brings them reward. —PROVERBS 12:14

From time to time we all get overheated about things that are not a crisis but feel like one in that moment. In my family, when these types of life events happen, we have a tendency to assume the worst before getting all the facts. This happens enough that I've developed a response designed to cut the tension.

When "disaster" strikes, I call out, "Okay, guys, first, let's panic." I get blank stares. "Come on, we can do better than that. Let's panic." More stares. "Okay, now that we've gotten that out of the way, what should we do about this issue?"

I always think I'm hilariously funny in doing this. I'm not sure my family agrees, but I find it funny because it is so true. In the real challenges of life, the least productive thing we can do is to panic and let our overreaction get the best of us.

I share this because the same thing often happens in the career exploration process. Finding what we were built to do and love doing is all well and good until people start thinking about getting a job; then we break out in hives and run for the shelter of what we think is the nearest safe job field. How many parents have talked their children out of pursuing their true gifts with the dreaded phrase, "You'll never get a job"? How many Mozarts, Picassos, and Einsteins have we missed out on because they were convinced to "follow the money"?

Before you get nervous about where I am going, I want to reassure you that this chapter is about how to get practical and build a career that will earn you a living. Purpose and Inspiration are great, but if you try to use them in a way that does not provide value to anyone, you have missed the point. I do want to argue, however, that the correct order of exploration is to figure out your gifts and passions and match them with jobs that will reward you, rather than looking first for where you think the money will be and trying to make yourself fit. Here are three great reasons why.

Most Jobs Have No Obvious Path

When you find yourself in a friendly group sometime, ask everyone these questions: "How many of you, when you were in high school, knew that this is the job you would eventually have? How many of you knew that your current job even existed? Did any of you study in college or other training specifically for the job you have now?"

You will find a few people who have planned to be teachers from age six, but you may be surprised by how many people say that they stumbled into their current career. This is because most careers have no obvious path. We have so little exposure in our teen and young adult years to how many jobs are out there. The Bureau of Labor Statistics website lists more than eight hundred job categories—not individual jobs, but *categories* of jobs. The actual number of different jobs is too difficult to count. Most of us are familiar with only a fraction of these occupations. We assume that if you are good in the sciences, you can be a doctor or an engineer. If you like sports, your options are professional athlete or coach. If you like English, you'll need to be either an author or a teacher. But most careers do not have an obvious set of steps to follow.

My degrees are in international relations and history, but I've been successful in the field of higher education. This kind of thing happens all the time. We often have limited inputs when we make a first career choice. We look at what our relatives do, what our friends' parents do, and what we see on television, and then we make a guess. Unfortunately, if you limit yourself to occupations everyone knows—teacher, doctor, nurse, fire fighter, police officer, electrician, lawyer, plumber—you are eliminating most of the job market.

If you are preparing to make a first career decision, don't let fear force you into choosing something before you have done some exploration. There are so many opportunities out there that do not require any specific degree or training but do require energy and skills. The path may not be clear, but the rewards—both in terms of fit and financial compensation—may be excellent.

I have worked with many college students and recent graduates and seen where their work paths lead them. Sometimes students who pick more traditional paths experience less transition when they leave college and command higher starting salaries. Their counterparts who choose less structured paths may struggle more on entry into the market and have a season of defining themselves. Over time, however, this difference often evens out.

I frequently see graduates in traditional careers who feel stuck after three to five years in the field. Their initial salaries are high, but their income tends to stagnate unless they are willing to move or acquire new skills, and it is hard for them to make a transition into other fields. The less traditional graduates, who have picked up strong transferable skills, get used to managing their own careers and sometimes see greater changes in income over time.

Stay open-minded. It is great to be on a path toward a career that you know something about, but don't become so rigid that you can't react to an amazing opportunity that presents itself. God will often bring mentors or events into your life that will open a new range of possibilities that you had not considered. Be ready to make an objective assessment of whether that new frontier may be right for you.

There Is No Such Thing as a Secure Job

Often I talk to students who plan their majors around "where the jobs are." Their primary goal is not finding the right fit for their skills but entering a field where employment is secure. I try to warn them that there is no such thing. It sounds cruel to say that, but I believe it is important to recognize the truth.

When I started my career in higher education, physical therapy was a fast-growing field. Students flocked to it because of the high pay and the great job prospects. But so many students pursued it that within a few years the market for physical therapists was flooded, and new graduates found themselves without employment. In the mid-1990s, people were convinced that a computer science degree was the ticket to job security and six-figure salaries, until the tech bubble burst. Suddenly computer science grads had to go back to school to find new skills.

Where your talents and the needs of the world cross, there lies your vocation. —Aristotle[2]

Each time period has its "hot jobs." At that moment, we become convinced that those opportunities will never change, but they always do. Planning based on what is "hot" or "where the jobs are" is like trying to time the stock market—always a big risk.

This dynamic was even more clear in the 2008 recession. For decades, nursing and teaching have been seen as the most secure jobs you can find. School systems are always hiring, and the nursing shortages of previous years had created a wave of attention that led to sign-on bonuses for nurses and to school-supported graduate-tuition benefits for teachers. All that changed in 2008.

Suddenly hospitals didn't want to hire new nurses and pay their benefits. Instead, many paid overtime to bring their older nurses out of retirement to keep their experience and save money.

In the school districts, teachers who had planned their retirements suddenly saw their investment portfolios plummet in value and decided to put off retirement for a few years. The result was that colleges who had been used to placing 100 percent of their nursing and education graduates were suddenly placing only a handful. It was a complete turnaround.

That kind of change is bad enough for college students who trained for those fields because they loved them. Many of them had planned to be teachers or nurses since they were children. Eventually, the economy would turn around and they would get into the field they were so excited about. How would you feel, however, if you had given up what you really wanted to do because you were convinced that you needed a safe job in one of these fields? Uh-oh.

Industries change over time. Demand comes and goes. New technology and new patterns in the way we live are constantly changing the types of work that we do and the value that society places on that work. To plan based only on current trends is building on quicksand.

What makes a job secure is *you*. Companies seldom let go of their most valuable workers. People with great skills who can demonstrate that they can get results are always in demand. Job security is about being excellent at what you do, about constantly developing yourself professionally to make sure your organization can't live without you, and about understanding where the new opportunities are in the field so that you can make changes as needed. This is the process of identifying the E in the PIE principle—your Earnings Equation, which we'll address in a moment.

You Still Have to Manage Your Own Career Path

Thousands of jobs out there are still in development. Google's top-rated futurist Thomas Frey suggests that "60% of jobs ten years from now haven't been invented yet." Frey adds, "One of my primary complaints with higher education is that they tend to prepare students for jobs of the past. The way a Midwesterner would phrase it, 'they are constantly shooting behind the duck.'"[3]

How can you prepare yourself for jobs that don't exist yet? You can't. At least, you can't get specific training for the exact work you might do, but you can be prepared by cultivating the types of skills that you are most likely to need. In other words, you can learn how to learn. You can practice working in groups, managing projects, inspiring others to action with ideas, analyzing data, and many other crucial, transferable skills that will be in demand in the future.

The National Association of Colleges and Employers lists the skills and qualities employers want most. You may be surprised to see that none of these skills require field-specific training. They are all abilities that can be learned and practiced in many different areas of study and through a variety of life experiences. On top of that, most career experts predict that current workers entering the job market will change careers three or more times. Did you catch that? *Careers.* We're not talking about changing jobs within a field but moving to new fields three or more times across a working lifetime.

Building a career, then, is less about making one good decision concerning which job you want, and more about learning how to manage a portfolio of options. You will constantly face choices about whether to change your current job for another, whether to get more formal education or training, and whether to stay in your field or strike out for a new opportunity.

Sometimes you will be forced to change because of circumstances. Other times you will be presented with an unexpected opportunity and not know whether or not you should pursue it. Once in a while you may even get a nudge that you are in the wrong place, and that God has something different in mind for you. If you have only ever considered one career and trained for one job, how will you make these decisions? If you don't know who you are and what you were born to do, how will you assess if another job is a better fit? If you lose your job, how will you figure out what other options you have?

If, by contrast, you know your Purpose and your Inspiration, you can make an informed decision about your options by con-

---

**The Top-10 Candidate Skills/
Qualities Employers Seek[4]**

1. Ability to verbally communicate with persons inside and outside the organization
2. Ability to work in a team structure
3. Ability to make decisions and solve problems
4. Ability to plan, organize, and prioritize work
5. Ability to obtain and process information
6. Ability to analyze quantitative data
7. Technical knowledge related to the job
8. Proficiency with computer software programs
9. Ability to create and/or edit written reports
10. Ability to sell or influence others

---

ducting a little bit of research on the opportunity. In the future, we will all need to manage our portfolios of skills and career interests. You will need to know what you were built to do and what will inspire you to make an impact. You also need to understand what value you can bring to an organization and what it is worth.

Prepare Yourself

> Therefore, with minds that are alert and fully sober, set your hope on the grace to be brought to you when Jesus Christ is revealed at his coming. (1 Peter 1:13)

Ultimately, God is in control of our job security. We should always go to the Lord first with our concerns about making a living. Hebrews 11:6 says, "Without faith it is impossible to please God." In other words, what our Creator wants most from us is for us to trust God with the future. I once heard a very wise saint say, "There really is only one question in the universe: 'Do

I trust God?' All other questions are answered by that question."
Knowing that God has the future in hand frees us to concentrate
on the present.

This is especially true when it comes to our professional lives.
None of us knows what job changes we may have to make, how
many times we will change careers, or what difficult circumstances
we may encounter. Those we must leave to God. What we can do
is to prepare ourselves professionally to be ready for when God
places us somewhere. We can develop good professional habits,
practice building good relationships, and get as much experience
as possible in the situations where God places us so that we will
be well-equipped for our next assignment.

Ironically, this is also the best formula for making yourself an
in-demand professional. I said earlier that the only real job security is to be a precious asset to your employer (or to your customers, if you are self-employed). If you understand what needs
companies, organizations, and individual customers have, you
can learn to hone and market your skills in a way that makes you
difficult to replace. By making the most of every opportunity God
gives you to work, you can acquire skills and experiences that
help you fulfill your Purpose and follow your Inspiration with
greater effect.

> *Being busy does not always mean real work. The
> object of all work is production or accomplishment
> and to either of these ends there must be forethought,
> system, planning, intelligence, and honest purpose,
> as well as perspiration. Seeming to do is not doing.*
> —Thomas A. Edison[5]

How can you create this strong sense of value that keeps you
in demand and maximizes your opportunities? You must first understand what I call your profit center or your Earnings Equation.
You have to know what unusual skill you can provide with exceptional quality that organizations or consumers need. But you
have already spent time discovering your special abilities when

we looked at your Purpose, so now all we need to do is to match that gift with the needs of others.

When it comes to discovering the Earnings piece in your personal PIE, there are three steps:

1. First, we'll look at the idea of creating a personal Earnings Equation.

2. Second, we'll use the Options Matrix to start exploring careers where your Earnings Equation might fit.

3. Finally, we'll use the Professional Development Test to help ensure that you are headed toward the best fields for you.

Earnings Equal X

In order to combine your Purpose and your Inspiration in a way that is marketable, it is helpful to visualize a simple math equation. Using this equation will help you to talk about your skills in a compelling way, and it will allow you to concentrate your efforts on getting the education, experience, and training that will be of the most value to you in creating a successful and satisfying career.

Finding your Earnings Equation does not mean that your primary goal is to make money. If your goal is to do what you were built to do and what you have a passion for, however, it will help to understand how to make a living at the same time.

In light of your Purpose and Inspiration, what is the thing that you can do that every time you do it increases your economic value? Let's say you are a research scientist developing new prescription drugs. Every time you create a new drug that can be used, your value goes up. If, however, you are a research scientist using government funding to look for disease cures, your value goes up both when you make a great discovery and whenever you write a winning grant proposal that gives you more support.

If you are a builder, your stock goes up when you successfully get a contract on a project, complete the project on time and within budget, and do excellent work and win a referral from the customer. If you are a lawyer, you increase your value every time you win an argument or settle a case. If you are a doctor, your value is dependent on how many times you can correctly diagnose and treat problems. Professors typically find that their stock increases when they publish their research. Teachers increase their value by adding certifications, winning awards for creating curriculum, or using good teaching methods.

So what is the *action* that helps you make a profit? When you think about the Purpose that God has given you, what action can you take that helps others see how valuable it is?

My purpose statement is, "To help others see who they are and imagine who they can become." Every time I help people and the light bulb goes off for them—suddenly they can see how God made them and they can imagine how to use their Function—my value goes up. I've done this in different ways, sometimes through individual coaching, through teaching seminars, and through my writing. Whenever I do it, my Function is strengthened, and at the same time, more and more people recognize the value of what I do.

Again, it isn't all about monetary profit. If you are a minister, what is it that every time you do it, God's people are strengthened? If you run a nonprofit organization, what action do you take that inspires other people to get behind your cause with their time and monetary support? If you run a library or a school, what can you do that brings your organization recognition and shows your value?

The equation is

$$\text{FREQUENCY} \times \text{ACTION} = \text{VALUE}$$

Or

$$\text{EARNINGS} = \text{YOUR SPECIAL VALUE TO PEOPLE (SV)} \times \text{FREQUENCY YOU USE IT (F)}$$

Once you discover what your special value (SV) is, that is where you should focus your professional development. Be open to adding new skills to your portfolio, but continually sharpen your best skill—the one you were built to use. Think back to the analogy of a tool. If you have the perfect tool for a specific job, why would you choose to ignore its function and try to use it for something else?

You were meant for excellence. So much of the rest of the world wants to be good at everything, but we all know this isn't really possible. Honestly, we tend to have a few things that we do amazingly well and a lot of other areas where we are kind of mediocre. There's no reason to be insecure about that reality. That's why we need other people in our lives with other skills. I think God made it that way partly so we would learn to appreciate each other. Our Creator equipped us for excellence in unique ways that will bring God glory, so work from your best!

I have given you lots of examples here of different fields and what their Special Value action could be. You may not know your field at this point, but you can probably point to experiences where you were "on" (using your Inspiration) and where others recognized and received value from it (Earnings).

Maybe you love to inspire others and get them excited about an idea, and every time you get up in front of a crowd people tell you, "Wow, after you talked I was really inspired to go out and do something about that." Or maybe you are a quiet server who loves helping people feel better. People are always thanking you because you seem to be able to "anticipate my needs." These actions you take that receive a value response are announcing your profit center to you. All you need to do is listen and take notes.

Who Needs a Hammer?

Look back at your Purpose Finder results and your Inspiration themes. Which of your themes are connected with actions that consistently get outstanding results or reactions? They are likely to come from your Earnings Equation.

Take a moment now to look back at your purpose statement. What kinds of people and organizations desperately need what you are gifted to do? Who needs a hammer? What value could your gift bring to the following fields?

Education

Health care

Federal, state, or local government

Manufacturing

Technology companies

Nonprofit organizations

Retail stores

Service industries

Entertainment

Science

It may be difficult to imagine working in some of these fields, but there are probably jobs in each of these areas where you could increase the organization's value if you had the right training. Each of these fields has a different currency—a different way of proving its success. People in the entertainment industry get rewarded by the number of people they can get to pay attention; the science fields are rewarded for creating knowledge and making new discoveries; retail stores are measured by sales volume and the number of customers they can get through the door. How can your Purpose increase their currency?

Reread your purpose statement, and note the three to five fields where you think your gifting is most likely to closely align with how organizations get paid. How will you do this? By influencing people? By creating, improving, or repairing objects? By creating, expanding, or refining ideas?

In the Earnings Equation, SV (SPECIAL VALUE) X F (FREQUENCY YOU CAN USE IT) = EARNINGS, how would you describe your SV? Where do you want to offer this value? If you have no idea, start exploring by using a pair of free resources.

- **The Occupational Outlook Handbook** (www.bls.gov/oco). Here you can read up on what a job is really like through these exhaustively complete profiles of occupations from the

Bureau of Labor Statistics. You'll find insights into the salary, growth potential, working conditions, educational requirements, and working environment of hundreds of jobs that may interest you.

- **O*Net Online** (www.onetonline.org). This is another terrific government resource that helps people explore jobs. In particular, I recommend searching by the skills you want to use.

Managing Your Options

If you have some idea of what careers interest you, you are ready to start managing your options. When I teach career management, I have students complete an exercise that helps them think rigorously about the career options they might be considering. This is essential because we are not always good at being objective in our decision making. If we don't have a step-by-step process we either jump to conclusions without the necessary research or the options overwhelm us and we can't make any decision at all.

Sometimes one of my students will think of a possibility but immediately dismiss it because it seems impractical. Others could sit for an hour with a list of interesting jobs in front of them and not be able to rule out anything. The following tool, called the Career Options Matrix, allows you to put a defined process in place. If you work the process faithfully, I am confident that you will find matches.

Using the Career Options Matrix page, write across the top the names of all the jobs or job fields you are considering. A healthy number is four to six, but different people will have more or less.

Along the left-hand side are your knowledge scores. On a scale of 1 to 10, how much do you know about each of these fields? A score of 1 means you have heard of it but know almost nothing about it, while a 10 means you are currently working in it. A score of 2 or 3 might mean you've done some research. You might choose a 4 or 5 if you have completed informational interviews with someone in the field to learn what it is like. If you've completed an internship or shadowed a professional in that field,

Career Options Matrix (completed)

	(Career Field 5)	(Career Field 5)	(Career Field 5)	(Career Field 5)	(Career Field 5)	(Career Field 5)	(Career Field 6)
How much do I know about this field? (1–10)							
Benefits of this Field							
Negatives of this Field							
What would I need to do to start?							
Next Step for Learning More							
How much interest do I have? (1–10)							

Career Options Matrix (completed)

	Social Worker	Psycho-logist	Physical Therapist	Rock Star	Documen-tary Writer	(Career Field 5)	(Career Field 6)
How much do I know about this field? (1–10)	4	2	6	3	3		
Benefits of this Field		Help people, good pay, respect	Good pay, regular hours, sports				
Negatives of this Field	Stress, poor funding			No privacy, travel			
What would I need to do to start?	B.A. maybe MSW	Ph.D.	M.S.	Start tomorrow with band	B.A.		
Next Step for Learning More	Talk with social worker	Research daily work	Shadow a PT for day	Talk to successful musicians	Read occupational handbook		
How much interest do I have? (1–10)	5	4	6	2	7		

you might select an 8 or 9. Write in the score you think is appropriate for each job you listed.

Let's say my list of everything I've thought of doing includes social worker, psychologist, physical therapist, rock star, and documentary writer. I know some social workers and have spoken with them about the field, so I'll choose a 4. I've read a few articles about what psychologists do, so I've chosen a 2. I was injured playing inner-tube water polo and had to work with a physical therapist, so I've seen one in action. I choose a 6. Being a rock star sounds like fun, and I play in a group, so I'll pick 3. I'm a History Channel nut, so for documentary writer I give myself a 3.

In the next row down, list what you feel the positives of each job would be. For example, my research tells me that psychologists get a lot of satisfaction from helping people cope with the challenges of daily life. Perhaps I see that the pay is good, and that they receive a lot of respect as professionals. I note that physical therapists also get paid pretty well but still work regular hours. They often help athletes, and I enjoy sports. They spend more time actively moving around than sitting at a desk, which is a positive for me.

In the next row, write whatever negatives you know for each job option. For instance, the social workers I know always complain about being stressed, and they say that the agencies they work for never have enough money to serve clients well, which can be very frustrating. Even though there is a lot of glamour in being a rock star, there is not much privacy. It would be hard to be away from my family and friends traveling for long periods of time.

In the fourth row, assess what you would need to start in this career. Do you have the required skills and training to start tomorrow if you found a job opening? Let's say I have a four-year college degree. If I made the right connections, I could start creating documentaries or playing in a band. For social work, I could start in an entry-level job with an agency in some capacity, but I would likely need more education to advance. To be a physical therapist, a graduate degree and certification are required. Do I have the ability and the desire to get the training I need?

In the fifth row, record what the logical step would be for you to learn more about this career. If you are at the lowest part of the scale, it may mean Internet research or reading through an occupational handbook. If you are in the center of the scale, you should be communicating with people currently in the field and asking them what they like and dislike. Be sure to ask what skills you would need, always keeping in mind your Purpose. If you are at the top end of the scale, search for opportunities to get first-hand experience, which will give you the truest sense of whether this field will allow you to do what you were built to do.

There is one last row for a rating to be filled out after you take the logical step to learn more. Fill this out after you have done your research or talked with someone in the field. This time, choose a number 1 to 10 that represents how much interest you have in pursuing this field now that you have learned more.

Just thinking through these steps may have adjusted your interest level in some of the careers on your list. If an occupation drops below a score of 2, drop it from your list to make room for another potential job choice. If a score hits 10, that means you are actively pursuing it as a job choice. If a score is somewhere in between, start at the top of the matrix again and update your rating for how much you know about the job and then identify a new next step.

The power of this exercise comes from managing two distinct scales: the knowledge scale and the interest scale. As you take a next step in investigating any job on your list, your knowledge scale should increase as the picture becomes clearer. As your knowledge score increases, revisit your interest score. Would you say you are now more interested or less interested in this field? Take another step to learn more and adjust your score again. Each time you increase your knowledge, you will find you are a step closer either to confirming that career field as a viable possibility for you or to dropping that field from your consideration set.

Don't think of this exercise as a method to get to a right answer. Instead, use it as a tool to continually assess the options in front of you. If you maintain this list of options for your working career—not just until you get to your next job—it will help you assess whether you are in the right spot or whether it is time to learn more about new opportunities.

Take some time to fill it out now. What jobs are your current top contenders?

The Professional Development Test

The supreme accomplishment is to blur the line between work and play. —Arnold Toynbee[6]

To help you in the narrowing process or to assist you in confirming you are on the right path, I recommend using a little exercise I call the Professional Development Test. It is a simple exercise. All that it requires is that you look beyond your excitement at finding a new career and imagine how you would continue to advance your career five, ten, or fifteen years down the road.

Most jobs require some type of professional development. Some people need to take additional coursework or training; others attend conferences, write articles, serve on committees, take exams, or learn new technologies. If you want to advance in your field or even stay competitive in a changing market, you will need professional development.

Knowing this, the key is to ask two questions:

1. What type of professional development is required for the field I am considering?
2. Would I be excited to have this kind of professional development experience on a regular basis?

It is that easy. Professional development is at the heart of growth in any field. It is one of the biggest contributors to your profit equation. If that field is truly a fit for you, you should get excited about at least some of the professional development you have to complete. If you dread the thought of completing it, you are in the wrong field.

If you are thinking about being a scientist, a scholar, or a faculty member, you should enjoy conducting research and writing about it. If you want to work in the technology industry, you should enjoy learning about and experimenting with new kinds of software. How would you feel about learning new languages? If you want an international job, that would be a major contributor to your value.

The opposite is also true. If you don't like tracking progress towards goals, sales may not be the right field for you. If you are not willing to read up on the latest procedures and drugs, medicine is not for you. If you will fall asleep listening to new government regulations, skip accounting. If you'll go crazy attending trainings on best policy and procedures, don't aim for social work.

Apply this to the list of jobs you may be considering. Find out what type of professional development is required for advancement in each field by looking at a resource such as the Occupational Outlook Handbook, mentioned previously. Be honest with yourself. Does the type of training and development necessary sound interesting? Is it something you would consider learning or doing in your spare time anyway?

If you dislike the type of professional development required, you'll seriously limit your success in the field because you won't want to gain new knowledge or network with others who are interested in those subjects.

If you've worked through these steps—discovering your Earnings Equation, assessing your options, and testing your professional development scenarios—you should have a list of a few target jobs for you to manage actively. You may be able to reduce your list to one or two favorites. Now that you have all the PIE pieces of your Function, you are ready to put them together to take on the market!

NOTES

1. George W. Crane (1901–1995), quoted by Thomas Frey, "55 Jobs of the Future," FuturistSpeaker.com, November 11, 2011, http://www.futurist speaker.com/2011/11/55-jobs-of-the-future/.

2. Aristotle, 384–322 B.C., quoted by Larry Kreider, *Twenty-one Tests of Effective Leadership* (Shippensburg, PA: Destiny Image Publishers, 2010), 3.

3. Frey, "55 Jobs of the Future."

4. "The Top-10 Candidate Skills/Qualities Employers Seek," *Job Outlook 2013*, National Association of Colleges and Employers, April 3, 2013, https://www.naceweb.org/s04032013/top-10-job-skills.aspx.

5. Thomas A. Edison (1847–1931), quoted from Edisonmuckers.com, http://www.edisonmuckers.org/thomas-edison-quotes/.

6. Arnold Toynbee, quoted by Tammy McIntyre, "Create Your Dream Job," *Minnesota Spokesman-Recorder*, March 27, 2013.

CHAPTER 8

Storming the Market
Use Your Function to
Get a Job for Life!

It may be hard for an egg to turn into a bird: it would be a jolly sight harder for it to learn to fly while remaining an egg. We are like eggs at present. And you cannot go on indefinitely being just an ordinary, decent egg. We must be hatched or go bad. —C. S. LEWIS[1]

Whatever you do, work at it with all your heart, as working for the Lord, not for human masters. —COLOSSIANS 3:23

If you've worked through the previous chapter, you now have all three PIE pieces to assemble your Function. You can now answer our original Function questions:

Piece 1: What was I built for?

Answer this with your purpose statement: I was built to _____ _____. Imagine a tool, instrument, or object that might represent this. I've used the image of a hammer, but you might be more of a paintbrush or crayon that adds beauty to the world, or a ladder that helps others reach their dreams, or a golf club that sends ideas flying into the future. Be imaginative!

Piece 2: Where would I love to do it?

Answer this with your Inspiration research. What is it you never get tired of thinking about? What idea inspires you to action? Use your Inspiration questions to describe what kind of environment or industry would be best for you. Describe this in a couple of sentences: "I'd like to be in a flexible, creative environment that works with new technology," or "I want to work in some type of education-related organization that improves the lives of children."

Piece 3: How can I earn a living doing this?

Answer this with your Earnings Equation: SV (SPECIAL VALUE) x F (FREQUENCY YOU CAN USE IT) = EARNINGS. What is the skill (based on your Purpose) that you can provide to other people or organizations that they need? If an organization hires you, what will you help it do?

So for my example, I might say: *My purpose is to help people see who they are and imagine who they could become. I want to do it in an organization that focuses on developing young professionals. If you hire me, I will inspire your people to greatness and motivate them to reach your organization's goals.* That's the kind of statement that a hiring manager wants to hear.

Try your hand at combining your three pieces of PIE in this way.

Sometimes it can be helpful to give yourself a visual. My family likes to play a board game called "Who, What, Where" (University Games). You pick three cards that answer these three questions, and then you have to draw a picture that incorporates all three. Other players try to guess the answers. You might find yourself, for example, trying to draw Big Bird in a canoe eating a pizza.

Try this same game with your Function. Imagine yourself using your Purpose in your Inspiration environment and getting your Earnings result. Want some samples? Try:

- A person holding a calculator (I'm great with numbers), building houses (I want to make a difference with people who need it) out of dollar bills (by helping organizations raise or save money)

- You in a coach's uniform (I want to use my coaching skills), leading a group of joggers (to teach people how to take better care of their health) on a track around a building (so that my clinic can help them get back to their normal lives)

- You beside a shiny filing cabinet (I love to organize) that has a person's picture on the side (working as someone's right-hand help), holding a box of love notes (providing amazing customer service)

Now that you know your Function (and have the next great *Peanuts* cartoon in your hand), you are ready to storm the market and find the right job for you!

Job Search How-to

As you've already noticed, this is not primarily a how-to book of writing the perfect résumé or interview tips. There are hundreds of books covering those topics, and online, as the saying goes, "you could swing a cat" and hit ten different tips sites. My approach in helping you do what you were built to do is more individual. I want you to search for the right job out of your strengths—out of how you were built. So let me look at a few of the most powerful tools I know of to help you with the day-to-day tactics of job hunting, and see if we can identify what might be the most effective job search techniques for you.

Networking

Networking is inviting other people to help you by letting them know specifically what you are searching for and asking for advice or contacts to help you discover job openings. Almost everyone uses networking to some degree in the job search. Any time you give someone your contact information or ask someone to keep you in mind if they learn of an opening, you are networking. Truly extroverted people, who are energized by being around others, often find this surprisingly easy. With a little bit of practice, you can learn to market yourself with positive energy and a sense of humor that makes others want to help you and broadens your ability to learn of openings when they occur.

Informational Interviewing

If you are comfortable talking with people one on one, but the idea of asking someone directly to help you in your search makes you a bit queasy, try informational interviewing. Make a list of individuals you know who work in your industry of choice, or close to it. Let them know you are job searching and ask if you can meet with them to do some research and learn more about the field.

Don't ask them for a job. Ask about industry trends and jargon that you should know to be successful in interviews. Ask for their advice about what you can do to strengthen your credentials. See if they will critique your résumé and make suggestions. If your conversation goes well, ask if they know anyone else you should talk to in order to learn more. People enjoy being experts, and if you treat them with respect they are typically happy to refer you to others and keep you in mind if they know of openings.

I think of informational interviewing as the king of job search techniques because you can't lose. If you get a solid job lead or good contacts, wonderful! If you don't, you have still learned more about the industry and received professional feedback on your résumé. It has the same kind of power as networking but is more accessible to job seekers who are quieter or fear rejection.

Web Resources

In most cases, your first move when starting the job search will be to begin researching online. There are a wide variety of sites available to help job seekers. Some are more productive than others. They don't have the same focus, however, so it is important to select sites that do what you need them to do. There are

- **job boards:** large listings of jobs in all categories (e.g., monster. com, indeed.com, simplyhired.com)

- **industry-specific web resources:** sites connected to associations or with jobs related only to certain fields (e.g., higheredjobs. com for higher education, www.apa.org/careers for psychology, jobs.marketingpower.com for marketing)

- **career advice:** sites that offer a range of job-related articles and information and may or may not also offer posting (e.g., about.com/careers, careerbliss.com, careerbuilder.com)

- **corporate websites:** the sites of individual companies you may want to investigate for employment

- **LinkedIn:** This website is in a category all its own. LinkedIn is the professional's social network. It helps you maintain your contacts, get introduced to the people your contacts know, and get recommendations and endorsements from those who know you. Use LinkedIn as a digital home for your profile. Join, or even host, LinkedIn groups to follow the latest trends in your target industry and broaden your network. Human resources professionals use LinkedIn to post their positions to a target audience, and LinkedIn will even send job openings to you based on key words in your profile. LinkedIn is an amazing gift to job seekers who love social networking or are more comfortable shaking hands virtually than in person.

- **prospecting:** Prospecting is a process by which you identify where you want to work and try to uncover openings that might not be obvious. You can prospect by sending letters or email directly to employers or contacting them via phone to ask about current or anticipated jobs. Prospecting is not for the faint of heart, as it often involves a high degree of rejection, but it can uncover an opportunity that has not yet gone public. Your odds increase significantly if you have contacts connected to the organization.

- **volunteer, intern, or temporary work:** If you can't walk through the front door into a full-time opening, try the back door to show how valuable you are. One of the best hires I ever made was an individual who started working for my organization as a volunteer. He asked if he could do an unpaid internship to learn more about the industry. After six months, he had made himself indispensable to our office. We hired him for our next opening. Companies also discover some temp workers that they can't live without. If you can prove your value, some companies will even create a position to keep you.

- **creating your own opportunity:** Sometimes your best option is to skip the traditional path and create your own opportunity. You may start your own company, or you may decide to become a freelancer, consultant, or contract worker and offer your skills to the marketplace.

Getting Focused

When you enter the job market, you'll find all these options and others. How should you focus your efforts? Many job seekers use the volume approach and try to do it all. But your time and energy are limited, so I recommend that you focus on the activities that are the best fit for your situation and your Function. Start by answering these questions.

Part-time Dream

You don't have to choose all or nothing when it comes to creating your own opportunity. In most cases you won't be able to build a business overnight, so why not try to blend traditional employment with your dream job? A young graduate I know was inspired while he was still in college to become a motivational speaker for young adults. That's a tough field to break into and pay the bills. It requires time to build up a client list, and it helps if you have written something people want to read. Rather than pursuing his dream full-time, this young man took a job working in student development, first at his alma mater and then at a community college in an area he wanted to live. He honed his public speaking skills by presenting to classes and student groups. He used his contacts through both universities to connect in the college circuit and book talks, and he used his extra time to write a book he could use to support his work. He is great at his day job, but it also fuels his dream job by giving him income and providing him with a constant stream of anecdotes and connections he can use in his own work.

Am I Changing Jobs or Changing Industries?

If you have experience in a current industry and are looking for a new employer, your search is likely to be very specific. Focus on industry websites. Maximize your reach by updating your LinkedIn contacts and reaching out to any recruiters who may be looking for you. In one of my job searches, I knew I was looking for a lateral move to change locations. I went to an industry event and introduced myself to people at the booths of all the organizations in my target geographic area. One of these organizations soon had an opening, and I already had an inside contact, which helped me secure an interview.

If you are a recent graduate, this question becomes, "Am I looking for a job that clearly matches my degree and experience?" If so, I recommend spending most of your time searching for openings and making contacts within that industry. Make a list of your target organizations and get to know them by spending time on their corporate websites or social media pages. Use LinkedIn's advanced search features to see who you know who also knows someone at those companies or where other alumni of your university or high school work. Seek out advisors who can help you make sure you are ready for an interview, have great questions, and know the industry jargon.

If you are making a career change and not a job change, however, you will need to broaden your net and involve more people in your search. When employers see your résumé, they may not automatically know why you would be a good fit for the job. This is where having some contacts can make a difference. When you are trying to change industries, you are going to ask some silly questions just because you don't know the way that new industry works. Use informational interviews to get these questions out of the way. Informational interviewing will also help you build up a base of contacts who might know hiring managers. Their recommendations might get you in the door for an interview.

Joining associations or actively participating in LinkedIn groups can help you build your credibility in a new industry.

Career changers also benefit more from networking, as it allows their friends and families to become advocates for them in the search. Be specific about your job goal. No one can help you find the right job if they don't know what kind of job you want. If someone unearths an opportunity that is not exactly what you had in mind, you can always choose to be flexible, but telling your network that you want a job where "I can help people" might land you an interview to be a clown.

What Are My Job Search Strengths?

The Function you have worked diligently to find is also a great tool to guide you to the most effective job search techniques for you. Where are your strengths?

Purpose: What kind of tool are you? If your purpose involves motivating, inspiring, convincing, and generally connecting with people, you will find networking and informational interviewing relatively easy. If it involves serving people behind the scenes, look for opportunities to volunteer or temp for organizations so they can see the quality of your work rather than hear you talk about it. People who are built to work with ideas may find that joining or moderating LinkedIn groups will give them an opportunity to share those ideas. They may also reach out to thought leaders within the industry to find mentors. If you are skilled at working with objects, you should probably have examples of your work or a portfolio to show, and spend some time at events or industry websites to find others who share your skills.

Inspiration: It is always easier if you are searching for work in a field that is inspiring for you. Even shy people get animated and speak with more confidence when they talk about something they truly love. If you love the field, it will be easier to pick up the vocabulary from that profession and to find places where others who are passionate about it hang out either in person or online. Focus on industry-specific sites. Think about the products and services you love, and research the companies that provide them. Let your Inspiration shine through in informational interviews.

105

The people you meet with will be impressed. They will remember when they had that kind of passion for the field, and they will be motivated to help you.

Earnings: Knowing your Earnings Equation empowers you to manage your personal brand. Your brand is the promise that you make to anyone thinking of hiring you. It says, "If you hire me, you will benefit in this way: _____." What will you deliver if you are hired? Managing your brand helps you to create a consistent, memorable image in the minds of potential employers. It also makes it easier for people in your network to recommend you and to know how to help you.

May the Brand Be with You

You develop your brand in three steps. First you identify your positive features, then you translate them into benefits an employer would care about, then you provide proof points that back up your claim. It looks like this:

Feature: "I am a quick learner and efficient worker."

Benefit: "If you hire me, you will increase productivity."

Proof Point: "In my previous position, I helped my department increase productivity by 10 percent." (Include a quote from your former employer.)

One great way to generate the first part of the equation is to complete the following sentences:

I am a person who . . .

Someone with my values, strengths, and preferences could . . .

Success for me . . .

These are your features.

Now, do some research on your target industry. What are the biggest needs that organizations in your target industry have? Do the answers to the questions above help to meet those needs in some way? If so, these are your benefits.

STAR Technique

One of the best tools you can use to prepare for writing cover letters and for interviews is called the STAR technique. STAR stands for Situation, Task, Action, and Result. In interviews, you will often be asked, "Can you give me an example of your xyz skills?" The STAR technique (also sometimes called the SAR technique) allows you to tell mini stories to demonstrate your abilities.

Start by defining the **situation**. Let's say you had a summer job working at a flip-flop store at the beach. The situation might be that the store had seen a decline in sales this summer because a competitor's shop opened down the boardwalk. You discussed this situation with your boss, and she gave you the **task** of finding a way of bringing more customers into the store. Perhaps you took **action** by organizing a flip-flop fashion show and brought in kids, local sports stars, or a group of stylish grandmas to show how flip-flops can be more than just beach wear. The **result** was that show brought in an extra thousand dollars in sales that day, plus a spike in follow-up sales from the good publicity.

Sketch out a STAR story like this for each of your biggest work accomplishments to show that you know how to get results. These are the kinds of proof points that reassure hiring managers they are making the right choice!

Next come your proof points. Can you give specific examples of how you have delivered these benefits before? Did you improve an employer's process? Increase revenue? Save money? Receive outstanding customer feedback? Can you get an endorsement quote from a supervisor or use phrases from your performance evaluations to prove it? Do you have samples of your work, or charts or graphs demonstrating what you've accomplished?

If you are looking for your first job, you still should have some proof points from the classes you've taken, projects you've done, grades you've received on research, or results you've had from summer jobs. When has someone trusted you with big responsibilities? Why did that person choose to do so? How did you show you were worthy of that trust?

The secret weapon in creating proof points is to use numbers whenever possible. "Improved company sales" doesn't have anywhere near the punch of "increased profit by 10 percent for three consecutive years." How many people did you help? How much time did you save the organization? What volume of customers did you serve? How much difference did you make? Quantify your results, and you make them real to your listener.

Your Brand Statement

Craft these brand equations (FEATURES-BENEFITS-PROOF POINTS) into a brand statement you can use in multiple situations in your job search. It becomes the center of your marketing tool kit. A basic brand statement is three to five sentences but could be adjusted in length depending on whether you are using it in written form or as a way to introduce yourself verbally.

Here's an easy way to organize your brand statement:

What do you do (job duties)?

Who do you do it for? (stakeholders, customers)

Why or how are you good at what you do?

Why do you like doing it?

Why are you unique? What's your hook?

Give proof of how you have done your job well.

End with a call to action.

This framework clearly communicates your professional background and abilities and what you have to offer employers. Start by using it as a profile statement on your résumé, as in the following example from one of my job searches:

> Experienced admission professional with proven track record of progressive leadership and success in both highly selective and less

selective public and private environments. Demonstrated ability to build a successful recruitment team, create a customer service ethos that translates into enrollment success, cultivate strategic relationships, and manage staff and financial resources with integrity and effectiveness. Dedicated to helping institutions achieve long-term enrollment success.

This works well in written format, but it is a bit too long for a personal commercial—sometimes called an elevator speech—that you might share if you were meeting a potential employer at a job fair. For a personal commercial, you might start with something like this:

> I'm Susan Smith. I am a product/marketing manager with experience in managing products, services, and staff for a corporation. I directed a staff and managed the marketing of all company products.

Again, watch how I can improve it by adding specifics and a branding message:

> I'm Susan Smith. I am a sales-oriented ambassador for companies. For more than seventeen years, I have created an optimal mix of people, processes, and products for company success. I have developed marketing programs for more than fifty new products, more than doubled the top and bottom line revenue of my division at two different companies, and increased customer satisfaction with my current division by 50 percent.

Spend time practicing your commercial. When you use it, you won't want to say it word for word, but if you know it well, you can concentrate on how you deliver your message rather than just trying to remember the words you want to say. Having it in memory allows you to be more fluid and to pay attention to how your message is being received.

The same principle behind your elevator speech can be used elegantly when you are networking for job leads. You want to help your contacts work for you. To do that, you have to communicate clearly who you are and what you are looking for, while also helping your contacts understand why you should be considered.

Take a look at this script that I've borrowed with permission from career development Master Trainer Dr. Constance Jenkins-Pritchard. This is the kind of brand information you want to have ready for a conversation with an important contact who you hope will be willing to refer you to someone in your desired field.

> My name is (name). For the last (number) years I have been working as a (function) professional in (the industry). Most recently I have served as (level, functional title) at (company name), a (description of organization if helpful).
>
> During my career I have developed skills and strengths in (skill 1), (skill 2), and (skill 3). Currently I am in the job market because (my job was eliminated / my company is going through an organization restructure / I want to relocate / I am ready for additional responsibility, etc.). At this point in my work life I am looking for an opportunity to use my (skill), (skill), and (skill) in an area such as (example).
>
> I am interested in talking to people in (X industry) to learn as much as I can about opportunities for which I am qualified. Can you provide information or suggest contacts that would help me learn more about (XYZ)? Who might be helpful in providing information about (XYZ company)?

This is what I call a brand referral. It is sometimes also described as a networking statement. With this information, the other person has a clear sense of your situation and your goals. This makes it much easier for them to keep you in mind for opportunities and to represent you to others. Again, the goal is not for you to deliver this script verbatim but to express clearly the ideas listed here.

Managing your personal brand in this way is about telling a consistent story about who you are. If you understand your Purpose, your Inspiration, and your Earnings, this will be much easier. Your brand will also be exponentially strengthened if your image matches what you say about yourself. In particular, if you are searching for professional positions, build yourself a brand tool kit.

Your brand tool kit would include items such as

- A business card
- A professional-looking email address—not honeybunch@ yokel.com
- A one- to two-page résumé that has been proofed rigorously
- A portfolio that shows samples of your past successes (e.g., product samples, writing samples, charts of your results, brochures you have created, performance evaluations, letters of commendation)
- Professional clothing for interviewing and meeting contacts that is a fit for your desired industry
- An appropriate online presence on LinkedIn and social media sites (e.g., being on Twitter or Facebook is optional, but if you are, assume that a potential employer will check them before hiring you)
- A one-page list of professional references listed in a style that matches your résumé

For good measure, also do an Internet search for yourself using Google and other popular online search engines to see what the cyber universe is saying about you. Unfortunately, if the first entries that come up are not what you would hope, removing them is difficult. The best option is typically to bury them by adding more recent, positive entries on top. Start a blog and post professional material. Publish an article. LinkedIn profiles typically rank near the top of the pages associated with a name, so make sure your LinkedIn page is well-crafted.

Imagine you are the employer. You are not hiring primarily a person; you are trying to fill a need that your organization has. To do that, you need to ask, "Is this person able to do the job? Is he or she willing to do what it takes to solve my problem? Will this person be a good fit with my team? How long will it take me to train him or her? If I hire this person, will my life get better or worse?"

As a job seeker or career changer, it is your job to answer those questions. Because you know what you were built to do, you can talk about your passion for doing it and what value it brings to organizations. Your Function will help you answer with confidence. (For suggestions of great interview questions, see "Ask Great Interview Questions to Land the Job," a free resource at my site, www.aaronbasko.com.)

The Divine Headhunter

I've given you a host of action steps to use in your job search, but I have saved my most important piece of advice for last. I spent the first few chapters of this book trying to help you see that when you discover your Function and live from it, whether on the job or off, God gets glory and you benefit. The natural temptation, however, is to say, "That is great. I've got the theory. Now I'm going to go out and make this happen. I'm going to go out and get myself a job." If that happens, I have failed in my Function.

I have failed because I have not yet convinced you that pursuing your Function, particularly in the workplace, is a God-centered endeavor. If we do this right, it is not about us reading the instruction manual and then acting as if God doesn't exist. Instead, we realize that just as God has built us with a Function, so God is also the power behind teaching us to use it.

To go back to the analogy, we are the hammer that pounds nails, but God is the arm that swings. God already has job sites in mind, and we do best if we walk in partnership to find them. In an earlier book, *Help Wanted: Devotions for Job Seekers*, I wrote about God as the divine Headhunter.

> In your job search, you may have opportunities to make contacts with recruiters, network services, or career counselors. These can all be great resources, and God may use them to open doors for you or give you good advice. The Lord is a master at putting just the right people together for the good of everyone involved. Look for opportunities to build relationships with those who can impact your life and give you good counsel.

Ultimately, though, God is the best headhunter you could ever want. The Lord not only knows you inside and out (because, after all, our Headhunter is also our Creator), but the divine Headhunter, being omniscient, also knows the job market. The Lord knows what employers are thinking and when a position will open even before it does. In fact, God is the only headhunter I know who can actually create a position at will. God can accomplish more for us in minutes than a human headhunter can do for us in months.[2]

You are in the hunt for work that will be for your good and God's glory. That starts by letting God guide the job search itself. So charge into the job market, but don't go alone.

NOTES

1. C. S. Lewis, *Mere Christianity*, quoted from *Reflections*, C. S. Lewis Institute, Springfield, VA, May 2011, http://www.cslewisinstitute.org/webfm_send/232.

2. Aaron Basko, *Help Wanted: Devotions for Job Seekers* (Valley Forge, PA: Judson Press, 2012), 7.

CHAPTER 9

Surf Your Personality

Navigating Your Personality
in Changing Times

**When we are no longer able to change a situation . . . we are
challenged to change ourselves.** —VIKTOR E. FRANKL[1]

**"And no one pours new wine into old wineskins. Otherwise, the
wine will burst the skins, and both the wine and the wineskins will
be ruined. No, they pour new wine into new wineskins."** —MARK 2:22

What was wrong with me? Whatever it was had been creeping up
on me for some time.

I noticed it first in little things. One of my favorite activities
has always been watching movies. Movies have changed my life,
my vision of the world, and even my relationship with God. Typically two or three times a year, I would view a movie that inspired
me. I would get some startlingly deep insight from the story that
would change the way I lived. I would think about it for weeks
or months afterward. One day, as I was moving into my mid-
thirties, I realized it had been more than a year since a movie had
inspired me in that way.

I had the same experience with books. Since I was a kid, I
have devoured books. My first choices had been science fiction
and fantasy. In sixth grade, our teacher made us pick a book to
read to help us find new spelling words. I picked J. R. R. Tolk-

ien's somewhat obscure *Silmarillion*, a pre-history of the world of Middle-earth later described in *The Lord of the Rings* trilogy (think *The Iliad* meets biblical genealogy). It was a tome that most adults would avoid.

My teacher asked me, "Are you sure this is the book you want for your free reading?" When I insisted that it was, he relented. "Well, you won't have any trouble finding vocabulary words."

As I grew older, I moved from fiction to history, business theory, self-help, psychology, and religious topics. My in-laws still make fun of me because when I went on a first beach vacation with them, everyone packed their light reading. My choice was Henry Kissinger's *Diplomacy*, which was only slightly lighter than a concrete block.

Reading had always been a way to learn more about myself, to explore the mysteries of the universe, and to find inspiration. Around this time, however, I suddenly lost interest. Books didn't speak to me in the same way. My friends and relatives continued to buy me books. I would read the first chapter, skim a little bit, and then leave the book languishing on my night stand for months. Eventually I had a tall stack of books that grew too high to balance. All the books that typically would have interested me suddenly started to sound the same.

The scary part of this for me was that these had been some of the primary ways I related to God. Reading, studying, visualizing through movies, and savoring the deep mysteries of life were the ways I felt close to him. Suddenly even the Bible held my interest for only a few verses. I wanted immediate application. I went back and reread some of the inspirational books that I had considered life-changing only a few years earlier, but reading them was like drinking flat soda. I never lost my sense of God's interest and involvement in my life, but my traditional channels of communication felt like they had all been cut off.

Of course this affected my work, as well. Pieces of my job that I had enjoyed for years annoyed me, while I found myself drawn to new areas. These new areas weren't necessarily bad, but they were surprising and sometimes not in my core job duties. I felt more and more enterprising. I started to wonder whether I wanted to work for any organization or whether I would be best off figuring out how to work for myself. Most of my life I have avoided risks and conflicts that were outside my known areas of strength. Now I found myself pushing the envelope a little, allowing conflicts to play out, and sometimes even starting them when I felt that would be the most effective. I began to resent deeply interference in projects in my area. I became frustrated and sometimes depressed in my work, feeling like my organization wanted to pay me to be a professional worrywart. I looked around me and felt like all my colleagues cared about was making everything look shiny on the outside instead of making tough decisions.

To some of you, none of these things may sound that startling. You may be a natural risk-taker, entrepreneur, just-the-facts kind of person, but you have to understand that I was not. In fact, had you known me, you would have said that these things were the opposite of my personality. I had always taken on the role of diplomat: helping everyone to grow, focused on creating a positive atmosphere, certain that every situation could be a win-win. When my wife first met me, she wasn't sure she was interested because she thought I was "too nice." (Later she changed her mind!) The things I was seeing in myself were the very things I had always tried not to be in my earlier years, so you can imagine how I felt about it. I started to have an eerie Jekyll-and-Hyde sensation, as though I had woken up one day and discovered some part of my personality belonged to someone else. I was a little freaked out.

Almost everyone experiences seasons in life where a job you have been in for several years no longer seems like a good fit. Sometimes it is hard to tell whether the problem is that the job has changed or that you have. To make a more informed decision about whether to stick with your current situation or move on, it helps to investigate the source of your unhappiness. Try answering the following questions to help you pinpoint what is not working:

Is It Your Job or Is It You?

1. Are you working with different coworkers now?

2. Do you find yourself frustrated with tasks that you used to enjoy?

3. Has your supervisor changed recently?

4. Even when you are very busy, do you often feel bored with the work you do?

5. Have the rewards you receive (payment, bonuses, recognition, benefits, friendship with people in the office) lessened from several years ago?

6. Have you felt a strong interest in trying something outside your job description but within other areas of your current organization?

7. Do you feel that the expectation level has increased greatly for your work or that the risk of failure is much greater than it was previously?

8. Do you find yourself wishing you could have someone else's job, not for the money or prestige, but for a different kind of challenge?

9. Do you feel you have been less successful recently in your position?

10. Do you feel you have been more successful but care-less about your success?

The odd-numbered questions are change-in-job questions. If you answered yes to some of these, it is most likely your working environment that has changed. Perhaps this happened gradually, so that you did not notice, but eventually you began to realize you do not feel like you are in the same job any more. Now is the time to evaluate whether the job is still the right fit for you or whether the equation has changed too much for you to still be a good fit there.

The even-numbered questions are change-in-self questions. If you answered yes to many of these, but no to most of the odd-numbered questions, you are what is different. Your personality may be changing or your priorities are shifting. It still may be time to evaluate if this position or career is still the right spot for you, but spend some time understanding what is changing with *you* first so that you don't make a jump because your personal life feels out of balance.

Cured by Orange Slices

The clue that started unraveling the mystery for me was food. For most of my life I have been a food inhaler rather than an eater. I definitely like food, but other than a few exceptions (bacon, steak, and crab legs make the top of the list), I primarily eat because that's what you are supposed to do, rather than from some deep personal pleasure in it. I'm one of those weird people who think cheesecake is way overrated and can't usually finish a whole portion of a real chocolate dessert. But about this time, something changed.

For the first time, I started really noticing my food. I remember fixing a cup of mint tea, and instead of my usual practice of absentmindedly sipping while I was trying to complete some project, I stopped and drank it without doing anything else. I remember thinking, "Why have I never noticed how good mint tea smells?" I put my nose over the cup between each sip. Then I noticed that it also felt good to hold a warm cup of tea.

It was also around this time that I decided that my favorite sound in the world is the sound of orange slices being pulled apart. Seriously, have you ever stopped and listened to it? It is an amazing sound that I find it almost impossible to describe. I had to share this discovery with my children, who found it funny. They both began running over to me any time they would eat an orange so that they could pull the slices beside my ear.

For the first time, I was really tasting my food. Every dish my wife made became my new favorite. I knew something was wrong when I ate three helpings of a new asparagus recipe she was trying out and went back looking for more. That had never happened before with anything green. It was as if I was sensing minute details I had never noticed before. Sensing.

Then it hit me. This might be my midlife crisis.

That phrase has a lot of funny connotations. We picture the fifty-year-old bald guy who suddenly decides to buy a red convertible or date someone half his age, but there is some fascinating personality research around the concept of a midlife crisis. First of all, it often does not take place in a person's fifties. Let's be honest, if fifty were the start of midlife, that means we'd all be living until we were one hundred or older. In much personality theory, the definition of midlife varies, but it can often start as early as (you guessed it) the mid-thirties.

Second, "crisis" is an unhelpful term, because as I found out, your experience of crisis comes mostly from your reaction to it. How you choose to interpret this fork in the road makes all the difference.

Getting Temperamental

About two years before God provided my tea cup, the orange-slice revelation, and the delicious asparagus to give me some clues, I had completed a specialized career certification with a woman who had a lot of background working with personality development. As part of the training, she gave me an in-depth perspective on the Myers-Briggs personality type theory and on her experience working with many individuals in career planning. The way she explained it, personality type theory proposes that there are four basic tools for understanding and making decisions about the world around us. In the first half of our lives, two of these tools dominate. We are born with a first-preference tool, which is balanced out by a second. These two ways of looking at the world form the basis of our personality. Over time, however, and especially as we move into the second half of life, we experiment and become more comfortable with the other two tools.[2]

Another area of the theory suggests that when our personality begins to mature fully by bringing our least natural tool into the mix, we often experience a sense of personality friction that is the basis for what we call the midlife crisis. Far from being a breakdown or crisis moment, this is like a completing of our personality, as we begin to achieve comfort navigating the world with all four skills. Because we have seen life through a certain primary lens for so long, however, it can be an uncomfortable experience.[3]

Imagine what would happen if for the first thirty years of your life you wore a patch over one of your eyes that you lifted for just ten minutes a day to exercise the eye. Now imagine that after those thirty years, you suddenly switched and covered the other eye for half or more of the day, and relied only on the eye that had been previously covered. Think you'd be dizzy for a while?

This one observation may have kept me from going crazy during the time I observed my personality making radical shifts. I found another theory, David Keirsey's work on temperaments, even more helpful in applying this new insight. Temperament theory breaks people into four personality groups (as opposed to the sixteen-option Myers-Briggs model), so it sometimes seems a bit more approachable. Once you have a grasp of the main concepts, you can have fun analyzing your friends.

This is how I picture temperament theory. Imagine you have just invited a group of friends over for a board game tournament. You pick a game that is fun and interactive but something that people tend to get animated about. An hour into the game, temperatures start to rise and there is a dispute over proper application of the rules. Instead of jumping in with your opinion, you sit back and observe how the members of the group respond to the crisis.

It looks like you could sort the players into four categories. The first group is frustrated because they feel like others are bending the rules. They probably quietly tolerated it at first, but they've hit a breaking point. They expect that the offending party's behavior will be corrected or they may quit.

The group they are mad at probably doesn't see the problem. They are taking advantage of a loophole no one has seen before. The rules don't say specifically that you can't do it, so why the big fuss? If others want the rule, fine, they will find another way around it.

Two other people are trying to hold together the harmony of the group. They are negotiating diplomatically to keep everybody talking and painting a picture of everyone working together. They ask, "Why not find a new way to do it that we can all agree on?"

One other person is also observing, at least at first. Once she sees how the conversation is going, she jumps in with a strong, informed-sounding opinion and tells everyone that there is a better way to play which is more complicated. Why not try that way? You have the strong suspicion that this person is the only one to have ever played the more complex version and is likely to sweep everyone else from the board.

You have just witnessed the four temperaments in action. These natural tendencies are different ways of seeing and interacting with the world. Understanding the values of each temperament can often help you predict how people will relate to each other.

Keirsey says that each person has a preference in how he or she uses language. Some people see the world *concretely*. When they speak, they talk about everyday occurrences in practical terms. When you chat with a concrete language user, you may discuss the weather, clothing trends, what they ate at a restaurant, or what they bought most recently. If you can't see it, touch it, hear it, or taste it, you are not likely to hear about it.

Other people use language *abstractly*. These folks see meaning behind events. They recognize patterns and draw conclusions. They want to focus on the big picture, and they often notice how some things relate to other things. In your conversation with an abstract language user, you might talk about a favorite book or movie and discuss its similarities to other life experiences. You might talk about large cultural trends or discuss why certain types of things are better than other types. Typically, abstracts use a wide array of words and are descriptive as they seek to talk about the why behind the what.

Keirsey also divides people into two groups based on the way that they use tools. Imagine yourself in an elementary school. You look around at recess and see kids behaving differently. Some kids are careful to play by the rules of whatever game is picked. Even if they lose or the game is not working that well, they continue to play by the rules everyone has agreed to use. The rules of the game could be changed, but only if everyone agrees that the rules should be changed. If someone breaks the rules, those kids get upset and feel that the rule breaker should get "in trouble" in some way. These kids can be kind or mean, but they work within an agreed-upon framework and want very much for everyone to do so as well. They typically break the rules only if they are pretty sure it won't affect anyone else.

The other group of kids you observe seems to do the opposite. They tend to work around the rules. They will use playground equipment in ways never intended by the designer. They will change the rules or change the game if it doesn't suit them, or they will avoid the game altogether and go off to create their own entertainment. They don't seem to worry that much about hurting others' feelings. They may be kind or mean, but they can't figure out why other kids would stick to rules that seem dumb or ineffective. They take the straightest path to the most effective outcome.

Temperament theory labels the first group *cooperative* in their use of tools and calls the second group *utilitarian*. A tool can be anything, from a construction tool to a toy, from art supplies or sports equipment to the human body, from words to social rules. Anything that can be utilized or manipulated to bring about a result is a tool that the first group uses within agreed-upon boundaries and the second group uses in any way they think will get the desired result.[4]

If you can answer the questions "How do they use language?" (abstract or concrete) and "How do they use tools?" (cooperative or utilitarian), you can utilize temperament theory to understand why people do what they do. People who are concrete and cooperative tend to be traditional, faithful, practical, warm, loyal, and no-nonsense. They often make great teachers, nurses, office managers, and accountants. They value stability and focus on daily life.

Their opposites, people who are abstract in their language use and utilitarian with their tools, love to analyze things and pull them apart. They design and create elaborate systems and tend to be discriminating and selective in their tastes. They often have a dry humor and love to critique. They tend to be skeptical in their approach to life. They often come across as intellectual but are sometimes seen as aloof. Many college professors, scientists, engineers, and computer science professionals come from this group.

These two groups have a difficult time relating to each other. One group speaks concretely about practical things and expects people to play by the rules. This group values tradition and treating people fairly. The other group values lofty ideas and inventive thinking about complex systems that cannot always be observed or quantified. This group cares little for conventions or traditions if those guidelines get in the way of bringing their visions into reality.

The same thing happens with our other two groups. People who are abstract in their thinking but cooperative with tools are all about growth. They love to help people see meaning and purpose in life. They love to mentor, and they believe that each person should do everything possible to reach his or her potential. They deeply value harmonious relationships and want to ponder the meaning of life. These folks want to be counselors, teachers, and inspirers.

Their opposites—those who are concrete in their language use and utilitarian in their methods—don't want to be tied down. They are enterprising and often fearless. They walk into a room and want to own it. They tend to love competition and don't mind a little conflict if it brings good results. They often have fun breaking the rules and seeing what the outcome will be. They win at hands-on activities and often have superior physical capabilities. They pick up new tools of all kinds and are able to learn them and use them quickly. They often make great artists, entrepreneurs, and athletes.

You can see the conflict between these groups as well. The first group looks at the second and says "self-absorbed, rude, bully."

The second group looks at the first and says "wimp, dreamer, goody-goody." So who is right? Maybe both.

Hugging Mr. Hyde

How does this affect us at midlife? If age and experience bring experimentation, We should expect that as we move into the middle part of life, we will see changes. In fact, we should see traits that are the opposite of our primary personality style developing. Imagine that, for as long as you can remember, you have valued certain things, but at some point you begin to notice yourself attracted to the opposite way of thinking. The goody-goody starts to feel more aggressive and wants to do some muscle flexing. The independent skeptic begins to be nostalgic for his childhood and family. The hard-charging entrepreneur feels an urge to dedicate her life to a higher cause. The careful traditionalist starts loving games of strategy and thinking a PhD might come in handy.

This can be a little shocking. You start to do the things that have always driven you crazy in other people. You start acting a bit like the kind of people you have always tried to avoid. The result? Midlife crisis. You start asking yourself, "Have I gone crazy?"

Take a moment to review the list on page 125. If you resonate with more of those feelings than not, you may be experiencing a midlife crisis! The next move is up to you. Obviously, any of these traits individually can be simple changes in life circumstances that are not concerned with a midlife crisis. But if you find that many of them apply, your mind might be working hard to integrate new pieces of your personality into your old life.

Surfing Your Personality

Moe was a career engineer for one of the world's biggest companies. Brilliant, hard-working, and highly rational, Moe has always loved and valued his family, but when I knew him as a kid, the first word I would have thought of was "sharp." He seemed tough-minded, had a dry sense of humor, and high standards. Moe was the father of my best friend in high school, so we spent

---

Clues You Might Be Experiencing a Midlife Crisis

1. Your taste in reading material or television shows changes significantly.

2. You act like you are under stress even when you don't feel stressed.

3. You decide to make sudden changes in your eating or exercise routine.

4. People who know you well say you aren't acting like yourself.

5. You experience a strong urge to think about your legacy.

6. You have a desire to do new things that you know will get you into trouble.

7. You discover a desire for adventure.

8. You begin to have a feeling of being tied down.

9. You grieve over activities you enjoyed early in life that you are no longer doing.

10. You are surprised by a lot of things you never noticed before.

11. You experience major changes in sleeping patterns.

12. You find an increased tendency to blame other people.

13. You have a tendency to review and possibly regret earlier decisions in life that you thought you had accepted.

14. You want to spend much more time alone than in the past.

15. You have a persistent feeling that "I'm not the same person I was a few years ago."

---

a good amount of time together. He was the guy I went to when I needed help designing a product presentation that won me a scholarship to college. He was awesome in many ways—the kind of dad you respect for his strength, his self-reliance, and his ingenuity. But Moe was not exactly the teddy-bear type. He was direct and intense, with a skeptical eye and a no-nonsense demeanor.

By the time I got back from college, however, Moe had changed a lot. Still brilliant, as competitive as ever, and even drier in his humor, he had added something. When I came in the door, he wrapped me in a big bear hug, and he hugged everyone else, too. He smiled and laughed a lot more. Moe had new little grand-children, and he happily rolled around on the floor to play with them. At first, I thought of him as just more mellow, but looking back, my real sense is that his personality was more complete.

From my vantage point, Moe is a fantastic example of some-one who navigated personality development with style. He was able to keep the best of his personality type from early in life, but he added to it pieces he chose from other personality styles. His original temperament would clearly have been what Keirsey labeled a Rational—loving abstract language and concepts and using tools in the most effective way to build great things. As he moved into the second half of his life, he adopted some of the traits from the opposite temperament (what Keirsey calls a Guardian). Day-to-day family life became more important, as did

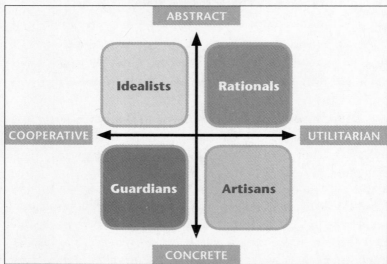

Temperament Matrix

traditional values and trusted friendships. He surfed midlife and landed the wave in style.

My own personality development spans Keirsey's other two quadrants. My temperament is what he would call the Idealist. Idealists use big ideas (abstract language) to help people (cooperative tool use) grow and develop their potential. Idealists love symbols and find deep meaning in everything. We love to inspire people, but we want to do it in an environment where everyone is in harmony.

As my personality continued to develop, I started noticing traits from the opposite quadrant creeping in. Once in a while, I'd find myself saying, "This 'unwritten rule' makes no sense. I don't think it should apply to me. Why do I care what people think?" I'd sense conflict between the part of me that wanted to be diplomatic and the part of me that thought the situation was dumb. Sometimes I'd find myself eager for a little healthy competition (that's weird), or I'd make a little more of an issue out of something because I felt a point had to be made (is that wrong?). I started wondering, "Why am I working so hard for someone else all the time? Maybe I should put some effort into solo projects."

This type of thinking is more like the Artisan temperament. Artisans live in the concrete world (hence my sudden interest in orange slices and tea), and they use tools amazingly well. In fact, they typically have few qualms about using whatever tool would be most effective. (If I need to get a little angry to get someone's attention, so be it. Nothing personal.) This was unfamiliar territory for me.

I definitely spent some time wondering, "Is it okay to feel this way?" But God threw me a life preserver in the form of personality theory. Things started to make sense, and I recognized I had a choice to make. I could say no to my midlife crisis, dig in my heels, and try to stay who I had always been. That would mean going back to the same old wells over and over again, telling myself that this time I would find fresh water and new inspiration. I would beat myself up when I felt drawn to being that kind of person I had tried to avoid as long as I could remember.

Or, I could choose to surf my personality. I could keep hold of the things I liked best of my Idealist temperament but sample its opposite and figure out what was worth adding. I could decide to taste my food rather than wolfing it down. I could break a few conventions and see if anything fell apart. I could take some risks on entrepreneurial ideas. I could sit and listen to the sound of orange slices.

I decided to surf, and once I did, midlife went from a crisis to a fantastic experiment. It was like having a new set of eyes, or discovering that there was a second room to the buffet. I remember describing how I felt to a friend. "It is as if my life up to this point has been me underwater, kicking toward the light. Now my head has broken the surface. I'm taking in a huge breath and looking around, wondering which way I want to swim."

Open Your Eyes!

It is worth the time to learn your temperament. Keirsey.com offers a free online tool called the Temperament Sorter™ that you can use to get started. The website also provides good descriptions of the basic temperament types. Quite honestly, though, if you enjoy a little armchair analysis, you can probably diagnose your own, just by asking yourself the following set of questions.

1. *Do I typically use concrete words (everyday facts and real-life events) or abstract language (comparisons, metaphors, ideas and concepts)?* Is your first reaction to this question, "What do you mean?" If so, it is likely that you use concrete language! Keirsey also estimates that as many as 75 percent of people are concrete in their language, so that increases your odds.

2. *How do you utilize tools?* Is it more important that everyone play by the same rules, or does it seem silly to you that people would do something other than what was the most effective? Is your motto "Let's just get along," or are you convinced that it's better to tell people when they are being foolish, short-sighted, or selfish?

If you can clearly answer these questions, you know your temperament. Now think about the opposite temperament and see if some of those characteristics seem familiar. If you are under thirty-five, pack them as a road map you'll need for the trail ahead. If you are over thirty-five, see if they explain some of the changes in perspective you have experienced.

As a side benefit, understanding the basics of personality type and temperament can give you an ace up your sleeve when it comes to parenting as well. Your kids will begin to display temperament characteristics very early in life. Once my son learned to tell time, he developed the habit of correcting those around him who were not accurate. I would say it was "quarter to five," he would say, "No, it's not, Dad. It is 4:38." He didn't do it in a self-righteous way, but he felt it was important to be correct. Once I realized that he was wired to feel that being accurate was more important than making someone else feel good, I felt less of a need to tickle him mercilessly when he corrected me. Understanding the personalities of my children, and recognizing the areas of conflict with my personality, has kept me from making a lot of parenting blunders (which is good because I find plenty of other ways to make them). Keirsey's *Please Understand Me II* has a terrific section on parent-child temperament and conflict, which was very helpful to me.

Walking with God at the Crossroads

The most important reason to learn to surf your personality, and indeed, the primary reason for this chapter, is to preserve and enrich your walk with God at the crossroads of life. This relationship, above all, will be affected by the changes in your personality over time. In most other areas—your work, your friends, even your family—you can fake that nothing has changed, but God knows you too well. If you are anything like me, you have probably developed your own most comfortable ways to relate to God, and midlife will shake them.

Imagine that you have had a best friend from high school who has continued to be a close friend into adulthood. You've built family traditions together and grown comfortable in your routines. Every Friday for the last ten years, the two of you have met for lunch in a favorite local restaurant. This once-a-week appointment has become central to your relationship. But one Friday, you eat the fish and wind up with a case of food poisoning. The next week you go back and notice that the dish you are served on doesn't look that clean. The third week, you are overcharged on your bill.

By week four, you've decided you don't want to eat at your local spot any more. You go a few more times, but your heart is not in it. If your lunches have been mostly about the tradition, you'll start finding excuses to skip them. You may start to wonder if it is best just to let the tradition go. You might even take a step back from the relationship with your friend. If it is not about tradition but about your friendship, however, you will call your friend and suggest trying another restaurant.

This is our dilemma with God at the crossroads of midlife. The way that we have always related to God seems inadequate somehow. We don't "feel it" in the same way. If we do not recognize that our personalities are changing, we'll be tempted to fake it. We'll say, "Reading my Bible in that way has always worked in the past. Maybe there's something wrong with me. Maybe I just need to try harder." We will try harder, and we will fake it more. It is like we are sitting in the restaurant with that friend, smiling and nodding but dreading the food.

If we recognize that we are developing and that perhaps the Holy Spirit is offering us new ways to relate to God, we will have the courage to ask if we can meet at another restaurant. If we ask, God may even recommend a new favorite.

This has been my experience. As I mentioned at the beginning of the chapter, I experienced God primarily through understanding and marveling at the big concepts. I loved God's mystery. I saw God in movies and books and in the great complexities of the world. Like many Idealist types, it was easy for me to imagine the spiritual world at work.

As I hit midlife, however, that shifted. It was like I was looking for God in all the same places, but God had moved on. At first I interpreted this experience as God pulling away from me, but as I began to understand what midlife was all about, I realized that the Lord was standing on the road ready to walk the next steps of the journey with me. I was the one stuck in camp, packing and repacking the luggage and whining because I couldn't find my divine Guide.

I am still growing into our new relationship, and I remind God often that I don't know what I am doing. I sense God less in formal, set-aside worship and study times, but more in normal "walking around" life. I used to hear God's voice most when I was reading; now I sense the Spirit more clearly when I am in motion—when I'm writing, for instance. The emphasis has moved from reflective to active. I sense that God wants to be with me when I'm drinking that cup of tea, even if we don't say a thing to each other.

This has been very humbling. I often wondered growing up why other people seemed to struggle so much to grasp faith and to believe in the world they could not see. I now realize that I had a natural advantage because of my Idealist personality (see page 126). I see that faith is more work through a concrete set of eyes. Yet that gives me hope that some of those I know who rejected faith early on may feel God drawing close to them in new ways as they age. Rationals may feel themselves drawn to the traditions of their faith and sense how real they can be. Practical Guardians may find themselves drawn into the Scriptures, exhilarated by wrestling with theology in new ways. The rough-and-ready Artisan may think about testing out entrepreneurial skills with a mission organization.

When this happens, we see what a truly incredible gift God has given us at midlife. Leave it to God to be too generous to leave us with only a half-developed personality. Our Creator allows us time to become the kind of person we are created to be. Rather than letting us get stale, God challenges us and invites us to be-

New Ways to Connect with God

Scripture promises us that God does not change, but as we go through changes, we see God from different perspectives. If you find that you are having trouble feeling connected with God the way you used to, try some of these new approaches.

- Try practicing some of the spiritual disciplines, such as meditating on particular passages of Scripture, fasting, or sitting in silence with God.

- Enjoy God through beauty. Look at great art, listen to classical music, watch some sunsets, go to the beach or the mountains, and ask the Spirit to show you more of God there.

- Spend more time outside. We often forget how well God is revealed in creation.

- Look for Christ in the heroes of stories. So many heroes of books and movies borrow their power from the story of Christ, our great rescuer.

- Make sure you are serving with your gift. Using your Purpose will make you feel closer to God if you do it in service to others. Don't keep it to yourself!

- Teach others what you know. At some point the disciple needs to also become a teacher, and we often learn more when we have to teach something.

- Stop trying. Sometimes God doesn't want us to do anything; we are only called to rest in the Lord. At those times, it will be enough just to know God is walking with us, even if no one is talking.

come fully grown children, sampling from all the gifts available. God won't let us settle down and pitch our tents only halfway through the adventure. The Spirit calls us on to know God in new ways. We are granted a new set of eyes to more fully comprehend God's greatness.

So if you are at a major crossroads of your personality, open your eyes and see the banquet God has set before you. Learn to surf.

NOTES

1. Viktor E. Frankl, *Man's Search for Meaning*, quoted by Alexander Vasely, "Biography of Viktor Frankl," *Viktor & I*, www.viktorandimovie.com/biography.

2. Katharine D. Myers and Linda K. Kirby, *Introduction to Type Dynamics and Development* (Mountain View, CA: CPP, 1994), 4–6.

3. Myers and Kirby, *Introduction to Type Dynamics and Development*, 30–31.

4. David Keirsey, *Please Understand Me II: Temperament, Character, Intelligence* (Del Mar, CA: Prometheus Nemesis Book Company, 1998), 27–29.

CHAPTER 10

Living from Your Function

Staying True to Your Purpose

For it is God who works in you to will and to act in order to fulfill his good purpose. —PHILIPPIANS 2:13

Fully to enjoy is to glorify. In commanding us to glorify Him, God is inviting us to enjoy Him. —C. S. LEWIS[1]

My family and I were visiting a national historic site recently. Nearby the national park grounds stood a small chapel—a monument to the heroes of that particular event. Most of my family took a quick stroll up the polished stone aisle of the chapel and moved off into the adjoining rooms. I walked to one of the front pews and sat down. The light filtered in from scores of small, ornate stained-glass windows that must have taken hundreds of hours of work. The front of the sanctuary was framed in stunningly carved wood and brass. Everything, from stone to wood to cloth, was of impeccable craftsmanship.

I'm accustomed to a very different decorative style in the places I worship. My first instinct was to see my surroundings as foreign or as simply historical. In many modern churches, anything too elaborate can be a bit suspect. We see it as unessential or showy. Then I turned and looked at my dad, who was seated across the aisle in another pew, clearly mesmerized by the strange beauty of the place.

"They gave their best, didn't they," I said quietly, trying to speak just above a whisper.

"Yes," he replied thoughtfully. "What do we give?"

"Not like this."

The care and the attention to detail were breathtaking. I could tell that many individuals had sacrificed years, maybe decades, to honor God by giving their best to this project. Others had given hard-earned money to support the masterful work I viewed all around me. They believed in this place, and they believed that they had found something worthy of their best.

Everything comes with a price. Living out your Function will also cost you, and the price is your best. You will confront uncomfortable risks. You will sacrifice, and at times you will wonder if you have made the right choice in following your Function. Toughest of all, if you really want to live from your Function, you will have to identify with it fully and let it shine. That will make you feel a bit vulnerable.

The special Purpose you have been given will still work far away from the giver, but the power and beauty of your gift is magnified to the degree you use it the way it was intended, which is to glorify God and to know God through it. You will not fully realize your Function until you are ready to give God your best. If you choose to use it first for yourself, or even those in your small circle, your Function will still slip out in small doses, but it will never have the effect for which it was designed.

In his classic work *The Pursuit of God*, theologian A. W. Tozer said, "Our gifts and talents should also be turned over to [God]. They should be recognized for what they are, God's loan to us, and should never be considered in any sense our own. We have no more right to claim credit for special abilities than for blue eyes or strong muscles. 'For who maketh thee to differ from another? and what hast thou that thou didst not receive?'"[2]

There is nothing wrong with making a good living using your Function. You should. Using that Function is what you were built to do, but your job should serve your Function and not the other way around. The highest purpose of your special gifting is not to make you money. The highest purpose of your economic work should be to give you opportunities to use your Function.

This dynamic can be tough to balance. When we find we are good at something that can produce income, we tend to strain forward and try to make it produce as much as possible. Industry is good, but if we care about our Functions only for the money they can produce, we have lost the path.

Once a month, ask yourself, "How am I using my Function? Who gets the glory when I use it, me or God? What motivates me to want to use it more?" Talk with God about it frequently. Look forward with anticipation to what opportunities God will give you to use your gift. When you feel yourself straining or getting frustrated because your Function does not seem to be producing results as quickly as you would like, "check yourself before you wreck yourself."

> *Mind, it is our best work that God wants, not the dregs of our exhaustion. I think He must prefer quality to quantity.* —George MacDonald[3]

The Yardstick Concept

We've already said that your Function does not dictate which job you will have. You can utilize the same Purpose in many jobs, just as the same tool can be used for many different projects. Your Function is transferable. You may also find that the match between a particular job and your Function may change over time. This can happen either because the job changes or because you change.

Although you were created for a Purpose, your understanding of that Purpose and where you should use it won't always remain the same. Indeed, that is one of the best features of basing your career and life decisions on your understanding of God's Purpose for your life, rather than on a set of skills tests. When you take a skills test, you will typically receive a long list of jobs that match your characteristics, but many of these will seem unrelated. (One of my lists included librarian, bus driver, and funeral home director—those seem pretty different to me!) How do you differentiate which will be the right fit? When you know your Purpose, you can use it like a yardstick to evaluate the many job changes most of us will face.

For example, my current job as a roller rink disc jockey is okay, but an opportunity comes up to be a director of a kid's campground. Do I stay or go? I know I love kids, and I get to work with kids in both places, but if my Function is "to help kids grow and develop their minds and their hearts," I should have more opportunities to do that at the camp. If it is "to help kids enjoy being kids" or "to help kids appreciate music," maybe I should stay. The point is, I should make my choice based on whichever option gives me more of an opportunity to fulfill my Function. Perhaps right now I spend only 40 percent of my time doing what I feel I was built to do, but I could be spending 80 percent of my time doing it in the new position. Which place will give God more glory and me more satisfaction?

*What is success? I think it is a mixture of having a
flair for the thing that you are doing; knowing that it
is not enough, that you have got to have hard work
and a certain sense of purpose.* —Margaret Thatcher[4]

Out from Under Your Bushel

"In the same way, let your light shine before others, that
they may see your good deeds and glorify your Father in
heaven." (Matthew 5:16)

I love to speak to groups. Some people fear public speaking more than death, but I find it thrilling. If I meet with someone one on one, I can act out my purpose statement to "help others see who they are and imagine who they can become." When I speak to an audience, this opportunity multiplies. For me, there is nothing like connecting with a group of people and helping them to glimpse how the mysteries of God peek through in their lives.

In almost every job I have had since college, I've had public speaking opportunities, and typically I've found them a joy rather than a burden. But one particular job stumped me. Several times a year, we held a large program that drew a big crowd. I was one of the speakers who would address the group. I knew my topic well and understood the crowd, but I was encouraged to play it safe in my remarks. My job was to not steal anyone's thunder. Once my speaking part was done, my job was to go and worry about the logistics of the rest of the day.

I dreaded these days. I ranked them in the top two or three things I disliked about my job. What should have been an enjoyable use of skills that were comfortable for me turned into a day when I worried about saying or doing the wrong thing. I was hiding part of my Function out of fear.

One day, I decided to do things differently. I dressed in my best, tucked away my conservative notes, and decided to go to the podium and be myself.

It worked. Beautifully. I spoke well. The audience was with me. I did not try to steal the show; I just spoke from my heart and my experience. The headliners did not seem to mind. In fact, I gave them a warmed-up crowd, and they spoke better than I had ever heard them. Best of all, I experienced no dread.

I enjoyed the day because I was living from my Function. Until that point, I was trying to present a truncated version of it, using my own skills to play it safe rather than letting God's glory shine through. You know the difference. When God's glory is shining forth, people look into your eyes and say "thank you," and you have no idea what to say. It isn't your skills; it is God's fingerprint.

When you are living out your Function, it often produces a strong reaction in others. If your Function is in an area of service, it may inspire deep gratitude in the recipient. If your Function is as a steward of some kind, deftly handling money or other resources, you may be surprised by the level of nearly blind trust others will put in you. This can be an excellent confirmation that you are doing what you are built to do. Embrace it, not by being proud of your abilities but by praising God and pointing others to the Lord as the source of your skill.

Don't be surprised if your Function also provokes negative responses with some people. You may be built to bring more truth into the world, and not everyone may be excited to hear it. This does not mean that you should look for opportunities to stir up controversy or conflict, but not everyone is excited about seeing God's glory shine through in the lives of others. Sometimes even a noncontroversial Function such as service can be taken the wrong way by an individual who is not ready to accept it.

Warnings for Your Journey

Speaking of negative responses, at this point in the book, it is only fair for me to warn you that there are some pitfalls that can derail you in your quest to follow your Function. So let me introduce you to a few.

Distraction

The best model we have of living from a Function is Jesus. It is clear from his actions and his words in Scripture that he spent a lot of time thinking about not just how he would die but how he should live. Just as we saw with Paul, Jesus had searched the Scriptures and found a passage that proclaimed his Function. Luke records Jesus selecting it for his first public message in the synagogue in Nazareth.

> "The Spirit of the Lord is on me,
>   because he has anointed me
>   to proclaim good news to the poor.
> He has sent me to proclaim freedom for the prisoners
>   and recovery of sight for the blind,
> to set the oppressed free,
>   to proclaim the year of the Lord's favor." (Luke 4:18-19)

Jesus' first message definitely prompted a strong reaction, and not one you or I would hope to receive. By the time he had finished, his hearers were ready to throw him off a cliff. This set the pattern for much of his preaching ministry. Even as Jesus proclaimed good news to the poor and oppressed, he spoke so directly that some people couldn't handle that much of God's authority coming through.

But Jesus knew his purpose, and he kept it directly before him. As Isaiah described it,

Because the Sovereign LORD helps me,
  I will not be disgraced.
Therefore have I set my face like flint,
  and I know I will not be put to shame. (Isaiah 50:7)

This clarity of purpose and calling allowed Jesus to resist the distractions that so often drag us away from our primary Function to other things that seem good but are not best.

Look at a story from Jesus' early ministry, recorded in Mark 1:36-38. After a long night of healing the sick, the next morning Jesus snuck off to pray alone.

Simon and his companions went to look for him, and when they found him, they exclaimed: "Everyone is looking for you!"

Jesus replied, "Let us go somewhere else—to the nearby villages—so I can preach there also. That is why I have come."

No one but Jesus could make it so beautifully simple. His work on earth was not to be a magician or get involved in local politics but to preach the good news to the poor. If others were looking to distract him from that mission, he decided it was time to go somewhere else. If only we could keep that perspective.

Think about it. What reactions have you received when you have tried to live from the Function God has placed in your heart? God built you to affect certain people in a particular way. When you are living from your heart, those people respond in a powerful, positive manner. But others who don't really understand your Function may want to misinterpret God's plan for you. If your Purpose is to find those whose hearts have been broken and help to mend them, those around you may say, "But surely that means only other Christians, or those in your own class or racial group, or only those in the United States?" When you follow your Function beyond their understanding, they may react badly. How have you experienced this?

What about distractions? When have you been tempted to dilute your energy from what you do best to other Functions you do less well? Imagine if Jesus had decided to preach the good news "on the side" and work on growing his healing ministry instead. Israel might have been free from disease but with no hope of a savior. This is exactly what happens to us when we take our eyes off our Functions and allow ourselves to be guided by the goals of those around us, no matter how admirable.

Seeking the Advice of People Over That of God

Think about how many people would be happy to give you career advice. Most of them think they are helping. Some are speaking from their own mistakes. Others find it safer to tell you to try something than to risk it themselves.

Author Timothy Ferris describes this as the "bike shed effect."[5] If you wanted to build a nuclear power plant, no one would offer you opinions about how to do it. They would recognize that it is a complex undertaking and that they have no real expertise. If you were building a bike shed, however, many people would be happy to tell you how to do it better, and to argue with you about all the details. Similarly, everyone who has had a job thinks he or she is a career expert.

Seeking advice from others can be wisdom if you find mentors who have experience with the same issue and understand your heart well. But too many people have also received bad advice when they have had tough career decisions to make. From my background in the college context, I would say that the overwhelming majority of bad career advice comes from well-meaning family members. You would not let Uncle Larry the accountant fix your carburetor any more than you would allow Cousin Susan the defense attorney to do your root canal, so don't assume either one of them will know your life's purpose. You must go to the Source.

In fact, to truly find where your Creator wants you, you must want God more than you want the job. To truly find and live from your Function, you must want God more than you want to know your own abilities. But the good news is that God wants to be found if we want to find God.

Proverbs 8:17 says: *"I love those who love me; and those who seek me find me."* As Ivan Veldhuizen describes it in his Ecipleship for Passionate Christ Followers blog:

> That phrase, "diligently seek me" comes from the Hebrew word "shawhar." This word most literally means "to be *early at any task, to be earnest or excited about an endeavor.*" The idea in this word is that you are so giddy about seeking, that you are energized to go after it as soon as possible. It's a little like the *fisherman* that rises at 5:00 a.m. to get on the lake, or the *deer hunter* who climbs onto his stand before sunrise. There is such eagerness for this experience that nothing can hold them back. The person who has this approach to finding God will certainly find Him. It's all in the orientation of our passions and desires.[6]

Pursue God with this kind of passion, and you will find that your Function and your job will be one of many side benefits.

Your Strength Is Your Weak Spot

Our victory is also our vulnerability. Our strengths, especially when disconnected from the wisdom of God, are also our greatest weaknesses. As author Holley Gerth describes it, "Your signature struggles are related to your signature strengths."[7] For instance, I have a great strength in finding the potential in others. That also means that I sometimes overlook when they need correction. You may be the opposite, with such a gift for identifying problems that need to be fixed that you never pat anyone on the back.

Our glory is our most likely downfall. When we start thinking of our Functions as ours, and not as gifts given by God, they have a tendency to get away from us. We are like the tragic Greek heroes whose consummate bravery quickly turns to hubris, and we end up being eaten by some one-eyed monster. Overreliance on your gift can also provoke frustration when that gift is not the right fit for a particular problem. If you are a hammer who loves to pound nails, you may occasionally encounter a screw. The temptation will be to pound harder.

Here are some tried and true tips for preventing your Function from backfiring:

- Be sure you have a least a few people in your life who will tell you the truth when you get full of yourself. Find one or two people who you trust who can lovingly pop the balloon of your ego when you need it. Consider these people your bodyguards.

- Stay connected with God, your source. Every few months, take some time and ask, "Am I still using this gift the way you want me to use it? Where am I missing opportunities?" Thank God for giving you the strengths you have, but be honest with God about the challenges your Function creates. God knows how you feel anyway, so you might as well be transparent about it. King David was a good model for this, crying out to God, even in complaint and frustration, as in Psalm 22:1-2:

My God, my God, why have you forsaken me?
  Why are you so far from saving me,
    so far from my cries of anguish?
My God, I cry out by day, but you do not answer,
  by night, but I find no rest.

See Psalms 38, 55, and 69 for other great examples of this. God is big enough to handle your concerns and doubts.

- Watch your stress. When you have pushed yourself too far, you will often act in ways contrary to your normal Function.

Under stress, the encourager becomes critical, the organizer feels overwhelmed, the server retreats into self-pity. When others begin to tell you that you are not acting like yourself, back off and get some rest.

- Check your motivation. When you feel like you might be losing clarity, ask yourself, "Why am I doing the work I am doing?" Be brutally honest. Are you motivated by the money? Is it prestige? The praise of others? It is not bad to be recognized and rewarded, but if those are your primary motivations, you are naturally more inclined to rely on your skills rather than God to get them.

Know Your Stress Signs

You lose your patience over small things. You bite your fingernails. You try to micromanage the people around you. We all have tell-tale signs that we have reached our stress breaking point. Learning to recognize these signs early can keep you from burning yourself out. What is the giveaway for you? For me, the first thing to go is the ability to keep my appointments straight. When I forget to go to a meeting I had scheduled, I realize that I'm trying to juggle too much and my brain isn't keeping up.

Often, stress brings out the opposite of your natural strengths. My mom is an amazing encourager—one of the best I've ever met—but she'll tell you that when she is stressed, she loses her compassion, and suddenly her encouragement comes out as criticism. If you are normally compassionate and patient with hurting people and their needs, you may stop listening to anyone when stress strikes. If your normal style is a can-do, positive attitude, you may suddenly start talking as if the sky is falling. Keep track of these kinds of signals and see if there is a pattern with your stress levels. When you start to see the signs emerge, don't push harder and try to outwork your stress. Deliberately slow your pace and do what you can to give your brain a little room to breathe.

Open to Where God Leads

I should be used to this, but I am still surprised when God turns barriers into blessings. One weekend, my family and I spent a few days in Philadelphia, Pennsylvania, with my parents. The time between our traditional summer and winter trips to my parents' distant home gets long, and we made a point of planning in a quick weekend get-together. My parents flew from their home in Maine to meet us in Philly, and we drove up and picked them up at the airport. We spent a terrific time together, exploring the historical landmarks and enjoying the many museums and restaurants.

We were not supposed to be there that weekend. That summer, when we were making our plans, we had selected the weekend before. It initially looked clear, so my parents purchased their tickets and we all marked our calendars. When I looked closely at my calendar later, however, I noticed a conflict I had not seen before. When I was unable to adjust my schedule, we had to postpone the trip a week.

What a pain! We had to start the whole planning process over again, get my parents' tickets changed, switch hotels, and readjust our itineraries. Grumble, grumble, grumble.

Guess what? On the weekend we were originally scheduled to take our trip, the Northeast was hit by the earliest freak snowstorm in four decades. Airports were closed and thousands of people were without power. It was cold, wet, and windy. If we had gone on that weekend, it is extremely unlikely my parents' plane would have gotten off the ground. If it had, we would have spent a miserably cold weekend in a snow-choked city.

Instead, the next weekend, the temperature was nearly thirty degrees warmer. The sun shone almost the whole time, and a gentle breeze tickled the stunning foliage. Our original barrier turned into a blessing.

The rest of the weekend offered more of the same—with barriers proving to be blessings. On the second day, we were clogged in traffic for about forty-five minutes, and we all started to lose our vacation spirit. When we finally pulled up to our museum

destination, two minutes after opening, there was an unbeliev-
able parking space waiting right in front. The next day, we were
forced to detour around a race and cut off from the most obvious
route to an aquarium. We pulled to a stop on a road closed by
police cars. I pulled into a parking space to ask for directions and
realized we were two blocks from the aquarium in a metered spot
that saved us fifteen dollars in parking. The race also apparently
kept most other aquarium-goers away for the first hour or more
we were there, so we had the penguins and sharks to ourselves.

It was like that everywhere we turned. It was clear to me that
God was making a point. What looks to me like a barrier, or even
a burden, often turns into a blessing with a little trust.

Case Study: A Life of Function

> For just as each of us has one body with many members,
> and these members do not all have the same function . . .
> (Romans 12:4)

In the great drama of life, some heroes have only a few lines.
One of my heroes was named Joseph, and he lived nearly two
thousand years ago. The Bible tells us little about his background,
other than that he came from Cyprus to Jerusalem. There he was
apparently introduced to the gospel message by the believers. Seeing the passion of the early church, he was moved to throw his
lot in with them, selling some of his property to give to any who
had need. From the early chapters of Acts, we see that this was
not uncommon, but Joseph brought something else to the fledg-
ling church. With all his energy, Joseph lived out his purpose on
behalf of the church with fantastic results.

In fact, so clearly did he allow his God-given Function to shine
that it became his name. We know him as Barnabas, and as the
Scriptures tell us, his name means "Son of Encouragement."
Clearly his ability to encourage (meaning "to pour more heart
into") was so evident to all that it became his identity. Barnabas
is one of my heroes because it is clear from Acts that while the
verses devoted to him may be few, he gave himself wholeheart-

edly to fulfilling his Function and to living out what God had created him to do.

I am also impressed by Barnabas because he remained flexible in his thinking and allowed the Holy Spirit to change his role as the early church grew. Barnabas's function never changed. His role was always to pour more heart into those around him: developing and encouraging them, strengthening them with his mentoring and coaching, challenging and stretching them. But Barnabas remained open to letting God tell him where, when, and with whom he would use his gifts.

Somewhere on the path of his life, Barnabas realized that his function was to be a professional mentor. We see this first in his relationship with Paul. Paul, then called Saul, had been the foremost leader of a reign of terror against the followers of Jesus. Acts 8:3 says, "Saul began to destroy the church. Going from house to house, he dragged off both men and women and put them in prison."

Suddenly, God intervened. In a dramatic encounter on the road to Damascus, the Lord reoriented Saul's life. But while his whole life and purpose were changed by seeing Jesus, the turnaround was so dramatic and so unlikely that the community of believers had trouble trusting it. Perhaps this was a scheme to infiltrate the church and identify its members for future persecution!

No one wanted to be the first to extend a welcome to the one who had caused so much anguish and who could be looking for an opportunity to strike. No one but Barnabas. Acts 9:26-27 tells us, "When [Saul] came to Jerusalem, he tried to join the disciples, but they were all afraid of him, not believing that he really was a disciple. But Barnabas took him and brought him to the apostles. He told them how Saul on his journey had seen the Lord and how the Lord had spoken to him, and how in Damascus he had preached fearlessly in the name of Jesus."

Like a true encourager/mentor, Barnabas saw Saul's potential. Although he recognized the danger, he could not help but see the possibilities. Barnabas trusted his instincts, and possibly the prompting of the Holy Spirit, and began mentoring Saul, who would eventually become known as the apostle Paul and far eclipse Barnabas in the reach of ministry.

Barnabas must have been respected for his choice to reach out to Paul. He clearly became an important leader within the church, as he was next selected for a bigger assignment—to mentor a whole church.

The church at Antioch was in unknown territory. Up to that time, the new faith had been intentionally shared only with Jews, with a handful of exceptions. But the new believers who scattered to Antioch found only a small number of Jews to tell. Instead, they looked around and saw the needs of Greeks and other Gentiles. Surely they needed a savior, too. The believers there began to share with all those around them, and the people of Antioch responded.

Here was a new development. Suddenly large numbers of new believers were added to the church with no background in the history or meaning of the Jewish faith that formed Christianity's foundation. Could a culturally mixed church stay true to the teachings of Jesus? Could "the Way," as the faith was called, be a universal faith open to all?

Once again, Barnabas stepped into an uncertain situation. Sent by the leaders in Jerusalem, Barnabas was charged both to investigate the new development and to encourage and to strengthen the church at Antioch to grow in its faith.

Barnabas was the right man for the job. He knew his Function: to see and develop the potential in the group of believers. Surely he must have found some activities and thinking in Antioch that were different from that of the church in Jerusalem. The wrong person might have focused so much on the differences that the Antioch experiment might have derailed. Instead, Barnabas focused on his Function, and the "Son of Encouragement" guided and strengthened all he found that was good. He shepherded and mentored with great passion and joy.

> When [Barnabas] arrived and saw what the grace of God
> had done, he was glad and encouraged them all to remain
> true to the Lord with all their hearts. He was a good man,

full of the Holy Spirit and faith, and a great number of people were brought to the Lord. (Acts 11:23-24)

Barnabas's role changed again a few chapters later in Acts. As the leaders of the Antioch church were praying one day, the Holy Spirit told them that God had a mission for the now-named Paul and his mentor, Barnabas. Soon they set out to bring the gospel to the surrounding cities of the region. During this trip, Paul's abilities shone forth and he became the chief speaker. Barnabas was a strong partner and refiner for Paul. At this point, his mentorship of Paul was in the advanced stages. He continued to challenge, coach, and support, but by the end of the journey, Paul had become a leader in his own right and no longer needed the same kind of support. Like all gifted mentors, Barnabas's highest reward was to see his mentee surpass him in influence and to launch him to greatness. It can be a bittersweet gift.

The journey had also given Barnabas a new role, however, one which a few chapters later would put him at odds with his former protégé, Paul. With them on the journey, Barnabas and Paul brought the young disciple John Mark, and they began to mentor him together. This arrangement was interrupted, however, when John Mark left before the trip was complete. This was a deep disappointment to Paul, and likely to Barnabas too, but the two men dealt with it differently.

In Acts 15, we are told that Paul suggested to Barnabas that they set out on another missionary journey to visit and strengthen the churches. Barnabas agreed, but

Barnabas wanted to take John, also called Mark, with them, but Paul did not think it wise to take him, because he had deserted them in Pamphylia and had not continued with them in the work. They had such a sharp disagreement that they parted company. Barnabas took Mark and sailed for Cyprus, but Paul chose Silas and left, commended by the believers to the grace of the Lord. (Acts 15:37-40)

What could come between these close friends? What would Barnabas feel so strongly about that he would break company with his former mentee? Paul's arguments may have challenged Barnabas at the heart of his Function—his passion to mentor others. The descriptions we have of Barnabas suggest to me that he was a good-hearted and positive leader, always seeking to bring believers together and create unity. But on his core belief in developing the potential of others he would not budge.

I imagine at some point, Barnabas must have thought to himself, or even expressed aloud, that Paul had been far less worthy of trust when Barnabas had reached out to mentor him. Now Paul was unwilling to take the risk on someone else who was in a similar position. Friendship clashed with the deeply held values of Barnabas's Function, and his Function prevailed.

So who was right?

Nearly twenty years later, as Paul writes from jail, he gives a list of personal instructions to Timothy, including, "Get Mark and bring him with you, because he is helpful to me in my ministry" (2 Timothy 4:11). Mark had indeed been worth the investment. Although the record is indirect, the best evidence we have points to Mark as the author of the second Gospel, which many biblical historians believe was written from the accounts that Peter shared with Mark when Mark served as his aide.[8] From Paul's letter to the Colossians, it is clear that Mark and Paul were restored to good relationship and that Mark supported and ministered to Paul when few others were with him (Colossians 4:10). Mark became an indispensable contributor to the life of the early church, and possibly the first Gospel writer, but none of this would have been possible without the mentoring of Barnabas.

Barnabas remained faithful to his Function, and he trusted the purpose that God had entrusted to him. Over and over he invested in developing others, even when the return on investment was questionable. Barnabas is an excellent example of discovering God's Function for you and living it out no matter what situation God chooses for you. Imagine what the New Testament and the early church would look like without the contributions of Paul and Mark. Imagine if Barnabas had not helped the church transition to including non-Jewish believers. This man's Function affects us all today.

Walking the Path

One of my favorite quotes of all time is from the 1999 movie *The Matrix*, starring Keanu Reeves and Laurence Fishburne. Morpheus, the wise mentor, tells Neo, the reluctant hero, "There is a difference between knowing the path and walking the path."[9]

This is so often our dilemma. Before reading this book, you may not have known what path you were built for and what you were supposed to be doing with the skills God has given you. If you have read thoroughly and done the activities, you now probably have a pretty good idea. Now the question is one of action. Will you be content with knowing the path, or will you take that next scary, invigorating step and do something about it?

I confess that I am still learning to walk and feel very much like a beginner some days. To quote another of my favorite films, *Luther*, "We preach best what we need most."[10] So it is with me. There are times when I forget who God has built me to be. There are moments when I am determined to work in my own strength. Yet still, I have made this commitment to move forward, to live from the Purpose God has given me, and to be a Purpose-finder for others.

I want to spend as much time as I can doing what I was built to do. I want to bring my two types of work—my job and my Function—together. I want to be effective in what I do, and I want to give God glory by living from the unique gifts my Creator has given me.

Earlier this year, my son and I were painstakingly cataloging my old baseball card collection. Most of the cards are not worth much, but their value goes up incredibly if they are autographed by the player. That insight made me think we, as human beings, aren't so different. Our value also comes from the fact that we are autographed originals, specially equipped, with God's priceless signature on us. We should display it.

I often think about C. S. Lewis's quote that "Fully to enjoy is to glorify." Living from your Function is one of the most extravagantly poignant ways to glorify. Giving glory with your mouth is one thing, but offering to be God's hammer, or screwdriver, or paintbrush, and allowing the hand of your Creator to move you is something else. Here we find our effectiveness and our joy.

We know the path:

> I know that there is nothing better for people than to be happy and to do good while they live. That each of them may eat and drink, and find satisfaction in all their toil— this is the gift of God. (Ecclesiastes 3:12-13)

> For we are God's handiwork, created in Christ Jesus to do good works, which God prepared in advance for us to do. (Ephesians 2:10)

Now it is up to us to decide whether we will walk it.

NOTES

1. C. S. Lewis, *Reflections on the Psalms* (New York: Harcourt, Brace and World, 1958), 90–98.

2. A. W. Tozer, *The Pursuit of God* (1948), chap. 2, www.theboc.com/freestuff/awtozer/books/the_pursuit_of_god/bless_possess_nothing.html.

3. George MacDonald, *Bartleby.com* quotes, George MacDonald, number 58, www.bartleby.com/348/authors/341.html.

4. Margaret Thatcher, quoted by Micha Kaufman, "Why Women Are Defining Successful Entrepreneurship," *Forbes.com*, April 13, 2013.

5. Timothy Ferris, *The Four-Hour Body* (New York: Crown Archetype, 2010), 195, attributed to C. Northcote Parkinson.

6. Ivan Veldhuizen, "God Wants to Be Found," *Ecipleship for Passionate Christ Followers* blog, July 23, 2010, www.ivanveldhuizen.com/?p=1303.

7. Holley Gerth, "What's Your Signature Struggle," http://holleygerth.com/whats-your-signature-struggle/.

8. John MacArthur, *The MacArthur Bible Handbook* (Nashville: Thomas Nelson, 2003), 315.

9. *The Matrix* (Warner Brothers, 1999), transcript, http://thematrixtruth.remoteviewinglight.com/html/transcript-of-the-matrix-9.html.

10. *Luther* (RS Entertainment, 2003), http://christiananswers.net/spotlight/movies/2003/luther2003.html.

Appendix
Discerning Function in Business and in Parenting

To learn and not to do is really not to learn. To know and not to do is really not to know. —Stephen R. Covey[1]

Function for Organizations

I was working with a Christian nonprofit organization that was at a crossroads. For decades this organization had been the outreach ministry of a community hospital. Its history and identity had been built on adding the "care" portion of healthcare for a medical organization. But the landscape had shifted. The healthcare industry had changed dramatically, and the hospital's ownership, leadership, and role in the community had changed.

Over time, this organization had responded to a few opportunities that were beyond its original scope. At the same time that its traditional roles shrank, its leaders received invitations to partner and serve in new ways, especially in areas of community education. Several of these experiments were successful, but there was always organizational tension, as leaders asked themselves, "Is this in our mission? Can we go in this direction and still be true to our history?"

My job was to help facilitate this conversation. The leaders and frontline staff gathered together with me in a conference room, and we burned through page after page of giant paper articulating what was at the heart of the organization. What we discovered was Function.

Just like individuals, organizations have a Function. In individuals, that Function is designed directly by God. In organizations, it is designed by human founders, but organizations can still serve divine purpose if we, as God's image bearers, are guided by the Holy Spirit in bringing the organization to life.

Again, paralleling individuals, the Function of an organization is not defined by its job title—the industry or category in which it is classified. It is defined by the organization's actions and the role it performs. That is what this organization discovered. As we talked about history and the accomplishments of which the organization's people were most proud, it became clear that the organization had not been created with a primarily medical mission in mind. Its champions were not doctors and nurses but helpers, talented coordinators, and advocates who could come alongside people whom the hospital either could not reach or could treat only superficially. Even when working with medical topics, this organization's Function was in the role of educator: helping people change their lifestyles and their quality of life through knowledge and service.

Identifying this Function made all the difference. Although the organization's core industry and affiliation might change, once the organization's members saw themselves clearly, they could confidently move forward knowing that they were continuing to serve consistently in their Function. In fact, clearly articulating that Function also had a practical aspect. The organization's leaders were able to use this understanding as a lens through which they could evaluate each new opportunity for outreach or partnership and then choose only those that were clearly in line with the organization's Function. This is the great power of finding your Function as an organization.

Hedgehog-like Clarity

Organizations are made up of individuals, and because of that they face some of the same challenges that individuals do. They must discover what it is that they are best at and seek to work from that core strength. They encounter many possible distractions and often find logical and good uses of their time and resources which nevertheless are not the reason for which they were created.

When researcher Jim Collins wrote *Good to Great*, his classic study of why certain companies achieved extraordinary success while other comparable companies did not, one of his key findings was that great companies developed what Collins called a "Hedgehog Concept." The name comes from an imagined battle between a fox and a hedgehog. While the fox tries every possible scheme to attack, the hedgehog curls into a ball and is impervious to any assault. Regardless of the tactic the fox employs, the hedgehog uses its one simple but startlingly effective technique.

For Collins, "The essence of a Hedgehog Concept is to attain piercing clarity about how to produce the best long-term results, and then exercising the relentless discipline to say, 'No thank you' to opportunities that fail the hedgehog test."[2]

One of the toughest challenges that both individuals and organizations face is the difficulty of saying no to good things in favor of the best thing. Time and again, I have seen nonprofit organizations chase after grant opportunities because that money seemed like the answer to their problems, only to find that free money was anything but free. In conforming to the grant requirements or in using the money received, these organizations slightly shifted their identity. They took their eyes off the mission, and they paid a price in opportunities lost. At the time, it seemed like such a small concession, but by doing so, leaders quietly sold the heart and purpose of the organization.

Businesses do the same when they partner with other businesses, or when they chase a new revenue stream without asking themselves, "Is this who we are? Is this the reason we were created?" Any opportunity that lessens the clarity of your mission is a loss.

Often an organization's Function was clear when it was first founded. The founders had a vision of what the organization would come into existence to do, and for a while they kept that vision first and foremost. Over time, however, that vision may

have faded. Perhaps the founders left the scene, or perhaps changing technology or changing business practices made the organization's original product or service obsolete. New structures,
services, and techniques were adopted, but were they adopted in
keeping with the organization's original Function?

If organizations wish to be successful and become satisfying
places to work, they must help individuals understand and utilize
their Functions. What's more, they must clarify their own organizational Purpose and keep that clear vision always in view.

In most cases, organizations are started for some Purpose.
Someone identifies a need that is greater than one person and
begins to bring people together to meet that need. Insurance companies provide customers with security and protection; medical
practices treat the sick; churches unite worshippers and equip
them to make disciples. In each case, there is a reason why the
organization exists.

Understandably, organizations change over time. People leave,
and the environment around the organization alters. These
changes often cloud the original Purpose of the organization, and
it becomes essential to clarify that Purpose anew. For an organization to work effectively, it must either reaffirm its purpose or
decisively modify it.

In many cases, the original Purpose is still the right one.
Thoughtfully revisiting the original intention of the organization's founders can jar an organization back into its true identity.
The organization might have to change how it talks about itself
or more clearly define which clients it will serve, but the original
foundation is given new life.

Occasionally, however, the landscape has changed so substan-
tially or the values of the organization have shifted so significantly that the original Purpose is no longer enough to keep the
entity thriving. Sometimes this happens prematurely. Companies
get so connected to a particular product or service that they provide that they come to believe that their Purpose is to produce it,
rather than to meet a need. They neglect the principle in Harvard

---

Ten Tips for a Better Strategic-Planning Process

1. Record your goals and guiding principles.
2. Envision the outcome.
3. Be specific and measurable.
4. Do the grunt work before your meetings, not during them.
5. Never come to the table without a specific agenda.
6. Show people you value their time.
7. Follow up immediately after each meeting.
8. Generate action steps from the ground up.
9. Keep momentum.
10. Use large-group brainstorming to sound out ideas rather than to generate them.

---

marketing professor Theodore Levitt's famous adage, "People don't buy a quarter-inch drill bit, they buy a quarter-inch hole."

To avoid this trap, organizational leadership must move the conversation away from "What product or service do we provide?" and toward "What role do we play?"

Five Questions for Recapturing Your Organization's Purpose

Use these questions as conversation starters to ensure that you are truly pinpointing your organization's Purpose.

What would be missing in our competitive market if our organization vanished tomorrow? For example, a bank might say, "There are other banks in the area, but if we were not here, there would be no institution with a focus on small businesses. We are small, and we understand small business better."

What would be missing from the community if our organization weren't here? For example, a local food pantry might say,

"If we did not exist, there were be no source of food help within a twenty-mile radius. Local churches would also lose a strategic partner in helping them fulfill their missions to identify and minister to the physical needs of the community."

Other than their incomes, what would be missing from your employees' lives if they were not working for you? A real estate agency might choose, "If our employees were not working for us, they might not experience the fun of helping people locate their first dream home or helping people confidently navigate the maze of paperwork that goes with buying or selling a house."

If we had to change our business model and could keep only one of these three things—the location of our business, the set of people we serve, or the product that we offer—which would we keep? This question helps you get to the heart of your organization's Purpose by asking the group to rank values. If your top value is your location, your real client is your community rather than your current customers. How could you broaden your customer base by strengthening your message about what you contribute to the community? If your top value is the particular segment of people you serve (bankers, families, churches), maybe your organization should think about what other products or services you could offer to be as valuable a partner as possible to them. If your organization's true love is the product or service itself, you should always be thinking about the next development in that field, and be flexible enough to follow the trends into new geographic areas or new customer markets. Your top value leads your messaging and your decision making.

If we were a tool in our customers' tool box, which tool would represent us best? Are you a wrench set, with a right-sized solution to every problem clients have in a particular field? Are you the level or plumb line that customers can constantly check against to make sure they are headed in the right direction? Are you an outlet tester, which alerts clients that a particular situation is dangerous and likely to cause them harm? Or maybe a saw that helps customers cut big obstacles down to a manageable size? Having a clear visual image of your organization's Function will help you anticipate how you can serve your clients better and how you can stay ahead of your competition or changes in the environment.

Answering these five questions should clearly illuminate the Purpose for which your organization exists. Examine the answer to these questions and pull out the common thread. Try to summarize your answers in a one-sentence purpose statement. This statement will serve you incredibly well as a measure for what initiatives you take on and which ones you reject.

If you have no compelling answer to these questions, chances are that your organization's original Purpose has drifted. You can reclaim and reinvigorate it, but there are two cautions. First, you must take stock of your external realities without focusing solely on giving the market what it wants. Second, you must have strong leaders, but the organization cannot take its identity from the leaders. The organization's identity must be larger than the personality or beliefs of a few individuals.

Start by going back to any founding principles that you may have on record. Try to reconnect with a bit of the original vision. Your business may have changed product lines or industries over the years, but it probably still tries to fulfill the same need. Milk companies may no longer need to bring bottles to individual houses, but they still fill the need of getting nutrition to people conveniently (it is a pain to find a cow every morning).

If you look back over all your products or services, what needs do your varied customers seem to share at a basic level? Sometimes interviewing your customers from different time periods can provide clarity. You may think you build flashlights, but your customers may think you provide a feeling of security. When you hear it from your customers, you begin to think of your organization's work more in terms of its impact.

Knowing what Function you fulfill allows you to look at the surrounding landscape and ask, "Where do we still see that need? Are there people who have that need whom we are not serving? Does everything in our portfolio contribute to that Function?" From this analysis, you can rebuild an identity that is purposeful and focused.

Function for Parents

Stay-at-Home Parents

One of the most consistent pieces of feedback I have received after speaking to groups is, "You should do a special session for full-time parents who are thinking about going back into the workforce." It is understandably difficult for parents who step off the career track for their kids to maintain a sense of their Purpose, Inspiration, and Earnings. In many ways, stay-at-home parents feel like these pieces of their personality go on hold when they focus on raising children. I don't think this has to be true.

As I discussed in previous chapters, your Purpose is not dependent on your job, nor is it defined by it. As a full-time parent, you definitely fit into my definition of the two types of work. Although you probably don't receive a paycheck, you clearly provide an economic benefit for your family and often for your community, as well. One good way to think about this is to estimate how much it would cost to hire someone to do the things you do. Childcare, education, home maintenance, food, transportation—all of these are costs. By doing these tasks, you allow your family to avoid the costs, which pile up quickly. You are effectively stretching every dollar of income. There are also many less tangible benefits, but clearly you are a major player in the economy of your home.

You also have the opportunity to do your natural work, your Purpose. Think about this list of Functions:

Customer Service Rock Star

One-woman Welcoming Committee

Makes Others Feel Safe

Idea Guy

Can Always Find a Deal

Prayer Warrior

Never Met a Stranger

Champion of the Weak

Your Personal Cheerleader

Shows God's Generosity

I Make Everything More Fun

Fearless Inventor

Any of these Functions could easily be used to strengthen a family. Any child could benefit from spending time with someone with these gifts, and with your gift.

Let me ask a couple of questions. Do you think that your Creator anticipated that you might be a parent when you were knit together in your own mother's womb? Do you believe that God intentionally matched you with children who would need you, specifically, as a parent? In other words, isn't it possible that God intended for you to use your unique Purpose and your Inspiration to be a more effective parent? By stepping into the parent role, you are not taking on a generic identity and leaving yourself behind. Instead, you are applying your Purpose to a new field. God has called you to a new construction site, but you are still the same kind of tool. The challenge and the adventure is figuring out how to use your Function in a new way.

Let's assume that my theory is correct, and that God intentionally gave you kids that are a match for you and will need what you have to reach their potential. Doesn't that change your task as a parent from "trying not to mess them up" to trying to figure out what that special match is between you and your children? What does God see that you don't yet see? How can you use your purpose to strengthen or teach your kids what they need?

I think one mistake we all make as parents is assuming that when we become parents we should suddenly be equally good at everything. Life doesn't work that way. Half the skills I'm trying to teach my kids I'm still learning myself. However, some skills I do naturally. It is easy for me to encourage my kids, to help them think about big ideas, to pass on a love of learning and growth. These skills are part of my Purpose, so I try to lead with them, assuming that God knew my children would need this when putting us together.

Over time, I have learned that there are other skills that I should not pretend are my strengths. In those areas, what I can model for my kids is that it is okay not to know everything. It is okay that we learn some things together and okay to ask for help. That is the perfect time to teach kids that God created them with a Purpose. "Yeah, God gave Dad a special Purpose to communicate with people, but construction projects aren't my strength. But see, God also gave Dad a friend like Mr. Mike. He can fix anything. So I can do certain things easily and Mr. Mike can do certain things easily, and God gets the glory from both."

You should also bring Inspiration into your parenting. It is good for your kids to see you get excited about something, especially big things. I joke with my children about how much I like bacon. Each year, my kids decorate with a theme for my birthday. This year they colored and cut out paper to look like strips of bacon to string around the room. My presents have included an "I Love Bacon" shirt and bacon duct tape. It is fun to have this running joke, but I sure hope that they see me as being inspired by something bigger than salty pork strips. I hope that when they get older they remember Dad for being passionate about helping others understand, about using the gifts God has given us, and about reaching out to people from other cultures. Show your kids that a new pair of shoes or the next football game is not a big enough Inspiration for a Christian. Teach them where your heart wants to make a difference in this world. Share with them your love of great books or art or restoring things. Let them dream big. Who knows what childhood Inspiration might follow them and help them change the world for the better?

Frequently, parents are unsure how to teach their kids about Earnings, or even if they should. I believe it is a great opportunity. Here is your earliest opportunity to connect your child's God-given gifts with the idea of work. While there should be some jobs that they do because they are part of the family, also look for ways to reward them for going above what is expected and fully using their gifts. In particular, reinforce that while anyone in the family can do certain things, there are some things for which they have special aptitude. These are gifts, and we have a responsibility to use them. It puts the parable of the talents into context.

> "His master said, 'Well done, my good and faithful servant. You have been faithful in handling this small amount, so now I will give you many more responsibilities. Let's celebrate together!'" (Matthew 25:21)

Above all, share with your kids that God has created them with a Purpose, and that part of the adventure of life is figuring out what it is. Tell them what you think your Purpose is and how you try to use it in your role as a parent. Model for them what it means to fulfill your Purpose beyond just a job. They will carry those lessons with them for life.

Parents of High School or College Students

As a parent, you have had an active role in your child's education, and it is natural to anticipate a similarly large role in your older student's career planning. Your son or daughter will continue to need your support in the career development stage, but possibly not in the way you might think. The career process is a perfect opportunity to practice the new relationship that will develop between you and your student as he or she enters the adult world.

When I am speaking to groups about career and college planning, I use a favorite example that I created to help families visualize how this process often feels for students. I call it the Train Analogy.

At some time, you've probably seen an action or adventure movie where the hero had to leap from the hood of a moving car onto a moving train. That is a little like how this process can feel. The moving car represents the momentum that the student has built up during the high school years from courses, learning activities, and accomplishments. Each student has an individual trajectory and speed.

Your son or daughter is standing on the hood of this car watching trains go by. Each train represents a particular career opportunity, complete with its own educational or training path.

As each train flashes by, he or she wonders, "Will that one take me where I want to go?" Each train also has its own speed. Some will get students to a destination only slowly. Others move so fast that a student not ready to jump is in for a hard fall.

So, what is a parent's role in this analogy? I picture the parent as the person inside the car holding the wheel steady while the student makes a good jump. Some parents make the mistake of climbing on the hood and trying to jump with their kids. When this happens, students lose their stability and typically make poor decisions, overpowered by the parents' influence. Other parents are far on the other end of the spectrum. They roll down the windows and push the student out! Needless to say, the student leaps without the support he or she needs.

I'm sure you are not either of these, but these extremes are good to keep in mind. After a recent talk I gave to a group, one mom approached me afterward and said, "I so appreciate your analogy. Now when my husband gets a little out of control in this process, I'm going to say, 'Get back in the car!'"

I share this because you hold a huge amount of influence, whether you see it each day or not. I have taught many college-level career planning courses, and my assessment is that most bad career advice is given by parents. This bad advice usually fits into four categories.

1. Follow in my footsteps. My experience is in this field. I know it and can make sure you will be successful in it. It has been good enough for me and should be good enough for you.

2. I made bad career choices or didn't have the opportunities that you do. There is no way I'll let you go into the field I'm in. I want you to have the opposite experience.

3. There is no way I'm paying for you to go into a field that there is no guaranteed job waiting for you at the other end. It is nice that you are interested in philosophy, but you will study accounting, nursing, or teaching. Those fields always have jobs (which is definitely not true, as the recent recession has demonstrated).

And the most deadly:

4. You'll never make any money at that. You should study business (or another "profitable" major).

Let me say from experience, you can wreck your child's car with these gems of advice. Students who spend three or four years of college studying what they are expected to do but what they hate typically do one of two things. Either:

They crash and burn in their senior year of college, hitting the panic button and realizing they need to change their major. This usually results in additional years of study or an unfinished degree. (Hear the giant sucking sound of time and money.)

Or, they follow through to graduation with the major they know is wrong for them, but then they flounder when they leave college. (Think years of angst, poor career decisions, and a possible move back into your basement.)

What is the alternative to these unattractive outcomes? I recommend that you focus your efforts on helping to hold the wheel steady but allowing your child to make his or her own jump.

What does that look like? Imagine yourself moving from a clear parent role to the role of a coach, at least in this area if not in others. Your new questions would be, "How can I encourage my student to use the resources available? How can I help by giving accurate, objective feedback? How can I help my student see options and learn to trust his or her decision-making ability?"

Good luck, coach!

NOTES

1. Stephen R. Covey, *The Seven Habits of Highly Effective People: Powerful Lessons in Personal Change* (New York: Simon & Schuster, 1989, 2004), 12.

2. Jim Collins, *Good to Great and the Social Sectors*, www.jimcollins.com/books/g2g-ss.html.